Teaching for Equity and Diversity

Teaching for Equity and Diversity

Research to Practice

R. Patrick Solomon
and
Cynthia Levine-Rasky
With the assistance of Jordan Singer

Canadian Scholars' Press Inc.   Toronto

Teaching for Equity and Diversity: Research to Practice
R. Patrick Solomon and Cynthia Levine-Rasky

First published in 2003 by
Canadian Scholars' Press Inc.
180 Bloor Street West, Suite 801
Toronto, Ontario
M5S 2V6

www.cspi.org

Table 5.1 is an adaptation of Janet Helms' colour racial identity charts, originally published as:
Janet Helms (1995). White and people of colour racial identity models. In J. Ponterotto, J.M. Casas, L.A. Suzuki, and C.M. Alexander, ed. *Handbook of Multicultural Counseling*. Thousand Oaks, CA: Sage. Used with permission of Sage Publications.

Table 8.1 is adapted from Table 4, "How the critical attributes pertain to each of the PDS functions," originally published in: Marsha Levine and Eleanor Churins (1999). Designing standards that empower professional development schools. *Peabody Journal of Education*, 74: 3, 4, 178–208.

Chapter 6, Cross-Race Dyad Partnership in Pre-service Teacher Education, is a modification of "Exploring Cross-Race Dyad Partnerships in Learning to Teach," by R. Patrick Solomon. Originally published in *Teachers College Record* 102, 6: 953–979.

Every reasonable effort has been made to identify copyright holders. CSPI would be pleased to have any errors or omissions brought to its attention.

CSPI gratefully acknowledges financial support for our publishing activities from the Government of Canada through the Book Publishing Industry Development Program (BPIDP) and the Government of Ontario through the Ontario Book Initiative.

National Library of Canada Cataloguing in Publication Data

Solomon, R. Patrick (Rovell Patrick)
        Teaching for equity and diversity : research to practice / R. Patrick
Solomon and Cynthia Levine-Rasky ; with the assistance of Jordan Singer.

Includes bibliographical references and index.
ISBN 1-55130-246-2

        1. Multicultural education—Canada. I. Levine-Rasky, Cynthia, 1958-
II. Singer, Jordan III. Title.

LC1099.5.C3S64 2003   370.117'0971   C2003-903526-3

Cover art by Alisa Singh
Cover design by Drew Hawkins
Text design and layout by Brad Horning

03   04   05   06   07 08   7   6   5   4   3   2   1

Printed and bound in Canada by AGMV Marquis Imprimeur Inc.

Canadä

Dedication

To our children, Christopher, Adam, and Elia, and children
everywhere, seen and unseen.

And to the next generation of
teachers and their struggle for social justice.

Table of Contents

PART TWO: RESEARCH TO PRACTICE

Better Prepared:
Putting Equity at the
Centre of Teacher Education

S chools systems across Canada have begun to experience something that they have not seen for more than 30 years—a substantial and sustained turnover of teachers. After two decades of political reforms, the profession is re-forming itself through a large-scale process of teacher retirements and hires of a new generation of young teachers. At this juncture, *Teaching for Equity and Diversity: Research to Practice* poses a critical challenge to the teaching profession, and most particularly to Faculties of Education charged with initial teacher education. As the 2001 census clearly shows (Statistics Canada 2003), racial and ethnocultural diversity is a fundamental element of Canadian society. This reality requires that all educators be prepared to live up to the responsibilities of a democratic vision and the mandate of public schools to challenge racism and ethnocentrism and to create an equitable future for all of our students.

In 2003, as this book goes to print, there could hardly be a more important time for all those associated with public education to re-affirm the democratic vision of the meaning and purpose of education. Across Canada the last decade has seen reforms to the public school system in the name of global competition and marketization. These reforms have largely put individual self-interest, choice, and accountability above notions of equity, social justice and a public good. However, the reforms have served to de-professionalize and demoralize teachers and to erode the democratic traditions of Canadian public education (Portelli and Solomon 2001). At the same time international events such as the attack on the World Trade Centre in New York on September 11th, 2001, and the American-led invasion of Iraq create new strains of racism within Canada. As well, these events underline the simultaneously local and global dimensions of a commitment to equity and social justice.

Public schools and their teachers have always been expected to serve many roles in Canadian society, but education—more than simply socialization, job-training or indoctrination—has consistently been held up as a central ideal. So too has the belief that public schooling should take seriously its *public* responsibility of accessibility, inclusivity, and equitable treatment of all of its students.

Much has been written about what it means to be "educated." Tom Simons, in a report on Canadian Studies in Canadian Universities entitled *To Know Ourselves,* offered a clear and concise definition when he suggested that self-knowledge lies at the heart of what it means to be educated. The development of self-knowledge, he suggests, involves a process of actively and critically constructing an understanding of ourselves as individuals and as members of a wider social and global community: who we are; where we are in time and space; where we have been; where we are going; and, what our responsibilities are to ourselves and to others.

For those of us working in the public education system, in a society in which social relationships are substantially mediated by race, ethnicity and other constructions of social difference, the ideals of accessibility, inclusion and equity make particular demands upon that educational agenda. We cannot justifiably allow only certain children to be educated—to know themselves in the fullest and most advantageous ways. Nor can we justifiably restrict some children's education by presenting them with restricted and "deformed histories,"— biased, stereotypical and limited presentations of who they are and what they can become. We cannot present some students with negative expectations and self-images. Neither can we permit only certain students the opportunity to actively and critically engage in the construction of their own identities and knowledge of themselves, while others have that knowledge imposed upon them in narrow and limited ways.

Rather, public education requires that our structures, curriculum, and practices at every level are informed by, and reflective of, the diversity of human knowledge and experiences in Canadian society. Public education must be committed to challenging practices inside and outside of school that unfairly limit some people's chances of being educated. Simply put, this is our responsibility as educators wherever we work within the Canadian public school system. Yet this is a responsibility that *Teaching for Equity and Diversity: Research to Practice* clearly shows we have yet to fulfill.

In 1972 the National Indian Brotherhood in its policy paper, *Indian Control of Indian Education* offered the following critique of non-Aboriginal teachers working with Aboriginal students: "... the role which teachers play in determining the success or failure of many young Indians is a force to be reckoned with. In most cases, the teacher is not prepared to understand or cope with cultural differences. Both the child and the teacher are forced into intolerable positions" (19).

More than 30 years later in a broader consideration of equity and diversity in Canadian education, this book highlights the same issue, and the lack of "preparation" is addressed in two distinct ways. In the first half of the book, "being prepared" to teach for equity and diversity education involves teachers' subjective interpretations of the significance of race and ethnocultural diversity in their role as teachers and their willingness to embrace equity and diversity education. In the second half of the book, "being prepared" takes on issues of prior experiences, in pre-service teacher education programs, that would properly equip the country's teaching force for the task of producing an equitable future for all students, regardless of race and ethnocultural identity.

The first half of the book discusses the findings of a national survey of Canadian teachers conducted in the mid-1990s, and its conclusions are depressingly blunt: "We argue that multiculturalism and anti-racism pedagogy has been slow in achieving the objectives of equalizing opportunities for racial and ethnic minorities because of educators' ambivalence, contradictory responses, or outright antagonism to the concept, policy, and practice"(8). The second half of the book, in sharp contrast, is inspirational. It draws on the efforts of York University's Urban Diversity Teacher Education Program and illustrates in great detail some key elements of a pre-service teacher education program that took seriously its responsibility to prepare teachers to work effectively for equity in Canadian schools.

This is not about adding a course about diversity into a pre-existing curriculum, tinkering with "special admission categories," or putting students into racially diverse student teaching situations and assuming that they will benefit from the experience. Nor is it about the agendas of individual instructors or isolated schools. Rather, what are presented here are elements of a comprehensive and sustained model of teacher education that is anchored in theory, focused on experience and critical reflection, and embedded in school and university collaboration.

Teaching for Equity and Diversity: Research to Practice provides a unique account of what programs in our Faculties of Education could look like. At the moment in time when a new generation of teachers is passing through these Faculties and entering the profession, the need for all pre-service teacher education programs to follow this lead could not be more urgent.

Jon Young
Professor
University of Manitoba
April, 2003.

Acknowledgements

We would like to acknowledge the financial contributions of the Federal Department of Canadian Heritage (Multiculturalism) in order to carry out the national study of educators' perspectives and practices of multiculturalism and anti-racism. We thank the Canadian Race Relations Foundation for its research grant to study teacher candidates' racial identity development and its impact on learning to teach.

Our thanks to Jordan Singer, for his extensive editorial assistance in reworking and fine-tuning the manuscript for publication, and to Elma Thomas for preparing some chapters and re-formatting the manuscript according to the publisher's specifications.

We are grateful to Jon Young, who supported this project from its formative stage and generously gave of his time to review the manuscript and write the foreword, to Cecille DePass for her insightful review of the manuscript, and to our colleagues Naomi Norquay, Goli Rezai-Rashti and Linda Richardson for their contribution to the alternative forms of professional development schools (PDS) described in Chapter 8.

We also thank the following publishers, who permitted us to include in this book materials that they originally published: Blackwell Publishing (Exploring cross-race dyads in learning to teach. *Teachers College Record* 102:6); Lawrence Erlbaum Associates for permission to adapt a table from *Peabody Journal of Education* 74 (3 and 4); and Sage for permission to utilize Helms' (1995) White and people of colour racial identity models, the *Handbook of Multicultural Counseling*.

We sincerely appreciate the integrity of the Publisher and the editorial team at CSPI in committing to this project. And finally, we wish to express our sincere gratitude to teachers across Canada who shared their insights with us, and to our research associates who collected and documented those insights and perspectives. More specifically, we acknowledge the work of Gary Bunch, who collaborated with Patrick Solomon in developing and implementing the Urban Diversity Teacher Education Program discussed in Part II of this book. We acknowlege, especially, the graduates of that program who have accepted the challenge of schooling for equity, diversity and social justice.

R. Patrick Solomon
Cynthia Levine-Rasky
Toronto
May, 2003

part one

Research

chapter one

Equity through Anti-Racism Praxis

E quity education is about hope. By engendering hope for a just and positive future for all children through equitable intervention in their academic lives, equity and diversity education has found expression in schools throughout North America, Britain, and elsewhere.

Forms of equity and diversity education are observable in educational policy, classroom practices, professional development, and in less tangible places such as individual attitudes and values. For who would be against a motherhood issue like equity? Desire for justice, especially when directed towards children, commands as much respect as any of the venerated values of our society. Indeed, equity and diversity education is an embodiment of freedom, individualism, mobility, and democracy.

Yet responses towards equity and diversity have often failed to move beyond abstract idealism indicated in the "shoulds" ubiquitous in educational forums. We have all heard these directives. Teachers should integrate equity and diversity education in all their activities. Schools should strive to reflect all groups in their displays, assemblies, and events. All children, irrespective of race, place of origin, culture, or religion, should be expected to achieve to the highest level of which they are capable. Educators should be provided with sufficient and meaningful resources to enhance their understanding of the social differences observed in their students.

All of this is good. It all logically and reasonably proceeds from a sincere wish to implement equity and diversity education in our schools. It all radiates hope.

The questions are how do we get there from here? How do we link hope to reality? These questions arise because we cannot travel far along the passage of equity and diversity education before we observe that the actual achievement of its goals and the hope we have for that achievement diverge—sometimes abysmally so.

This book is about that divergence. How wide is it? What is its nature and why does it exist? What are its sources? What do educators think and do about equity and diversity education, and why? What, exactly, are the manifestations of resistance to animating the hope that is equity and diversity education? What can be done about resistance? How can we talk about inequity while sustaining a concrete plan to realize equity?

Yet *hope* is the undercurrent in this book despite the often-discouraging discussion that follows. We believe that only with a thorough understanding of the divergence between the reality of the classroom and the hope for an equitable future for all children, can we reconfigure equity and diversity education so that it effectively addresses barriers to its implementation.

The passage is predictably an uncomfortable one particularly because our focus is on teachers' perspectives about equity and diversity education. This work is invested in constructive change, but it assumes that discomfort—even conflict—accompanies real change.

We can, however, successfully negotiate a way through the process if we continue to draw upon its underlying hope like a car upon fuel. All readers inspired by equity and diversity education should regard our objectives from this perspective.

RACE, ETHNICITY AND EDUCATIONAL INEQUITIES

Research has convincingly shown that members of groups identified by racial and ethnic characteristics experience educational inequity in our schools. Educational inequities for subordinate groups such as African North Americans, immigrants, and Aboriginal peoples[1] have received a great deal of documentation.

Rather than present an unwieldy review of relevant research, the hard facts are sufficient to command attention. To sample some exclusively Canadian data: as discovered by the Royal Commission on Aboriginal People, Ontario students are nine times more likely to complete their high-school education than Native students living in northern communities (Task Force on Indigenous Education 1991, cited in Dei 1994).

One out of every 33 Asian students was enrolled in a basic program compared to one in ten Whites and one in five Blacks (Toronto Board of Education 1987 in Henry, Tator, Mattis, and Rees 1995). In Toronto, 86% of black secondary school students were "at risk" based on their grades in English and math courses. This is a pattern that is repeated even when taking into account black students who have university-educated parents or parents in professional occupations (Toronto Board of Education Research Services 1991, cited in the Report of the Royal Commission on Learning, 1994, 93). Although 74% of all Grade 9 students were taking courses at the advanced (university preparatory) level, only 53% of Portuguese students and 61% of Hispanic students were doing so (Cheng and Ziegler 1993, cited in the Report of the Royal Commission on Learning, 1994, 95).

Henry et al. (1995) provide an overview of racism in the Canadian school system. In this text, manifestations of racism include attitudes and practices of teachers and administrators, Eurocentric curriculum, racial incidents and harassment, streaming, assimilationist culture, lack of representation, and devaluing parental and community participation. Particular examples include the labeling of children "at-risk," the delivery of inferior strategies of pedagogy for children in working-class and immigrant neighborhoods, biased assessment procedures with consequences of sorting children into various and selective educational streams, professionals with limited knowledge of ethnic and racial minorities relying upon psychological profiles and diagnoses that use biased instruments, and the perception of a general increase in racially-motivated harassment and violence in the schools. Even the provision of cultural sensitivity measures in the form of multicultural education is demonstrated by many researchers to be a form of discrimination and pedagogically unjustifiable (Jeevanantham 2001; Sarup 1991; Troyna 1987).

To discriminate against subordinate groups based on their putative attributes is to deny their equitable participation. Schools, as institutions responsible for the maintenance and transmission of a society's traditions, values, and norms, have shown tremendous partiality in the differential treatment of children. Those with the attributes most valued by the institution are favoured and benefit far more from schooling than those with other attributes (Curtis, Livingstone and Smaller 1992; Oakes 1985). According to Foster (1990), the structural inequalities of education affect the racial or ethnic minority students in several ways, including the evaluation of their academic potential, the curriculum they receive, the social relationship they develop with teachers and the career and life opportunities to which they are exposed.

EQUITY AND DIVERSITY EDUCATION

This book proceeds from the values articulated in equity and diversity education itself. Equity and diversity education is an innovation that directly addresses the issues of social difference and discrimination in schools and society at large. Educational jurisdictions in Britain, Canada, and (to some extent) in the U.S. have developed policies and practices to help eradicate harmful ideas and beliefs. The eradication of discrimination stands at the core of this perspective. The position presupposes the reality of racism as a dynamic interaction that thrives at the level of the society and at the level of the individual and everywhere in between. Barb Thomas, a noted anti-racism advocate, provides four objectives of equity and diversity education:

1. To explore the underlying causes of racism and ethnocentrism and its ties to practices and history that support stereotypes and prejudices, say, by critical examination of the accuracy and sources of misinformation about difference;

2. To offer an approach to culture that is dynamic rather than static. It takes into account not the overt manifestations of difference but "the oppositional elements which cause people to resist and challenge those things which hurt and oppress them" (1984, 22);

3. To support the effective transmission of "school knowledge" together with the lived experiences of children and their families, while considering as a matter of course the bias of classroom materials. It resists the temptation to evaluate manual and mental skills relative to each other and the educational practices which have been founded on such unjust evaluations; and

4. To link the ongoing and daily struggle of people against racist and ethnocentric activities on the local and global level.

In addition, Barry Troyna (1987) and Cameron McCarthy (1990) note that equity and diversity education calls for collective action informed by a political analysis of the way that racism and ethnocentrism function in society to exclude others. Implicit in these principles is an education in institutional forms of power that inform relations between dominant groups (as privileged) and subordinate groups (as marginalized) (see Winant 1997).

Equity and diversity education reverses the conventional organization of this system by centring the voices and knowledge of the subordinate groups. This is achieved, in part, by incorporating into the school program the experiences and expertise of people who are attached to students such as parents and community workers. The school program, in turn, is enriched through an acceptance of students' life circumstances, complex identities, and positioning in terms of broad social structures.

The project of an equity and diversity education, then, is to examine social and structural factors that create and perpetuate racism and ethnocentrism in society and analyze the ways they are transmitted, reproduced, reworked, and resisted (Dei and Calliste 2000; Foster 1990). We believe, along with many others, that changes to outward attitudes and behaviours are necessary but insufficient without a concurrent change in the underlying structures informing the way teaching operates.

Several issues require clarification. First, equity and diversity applies to all groups marginalized not only on the basis of race but also ethnicity, religion, and culture. While this text explicitly addresses issues of social difference along a race-ethnicity axis, we assume that our findings and approach are germane to other categories of identity such as social class, gender, sexual orientation, and ability and—in short—to social difference in all the forms in which it has been constructed.

Second, we assert that the rubric itself—whether equity education, multicultural education or anti-racism education—is irrelevant when determining educators' responses to the approach. Although the survey questionnaire used in this study queried beliefs about multicultural education (MCE) and anti-racist education (ARE), which corresponds to concepts utilized in policy documents at that time, teachers themselves express confusion about these terms and they struggle with sanctioned definitions. Policies, reports, and academic treatises adopt a plethora of terms in their versions of equity and diversity education. Policies may use the language of "race and ethnocultural equity" or more typically "race relations" rather than a discourse enabling educators to distinguish the one pedagogical approach from the other.

Some critics conceptualize MCE and ARE as innovations with different pedagogical and political objectives, classroom practices and outcomes (Dei 1996a; Mansfield and Kehoe 1994; Rezai-Rashti 1995; Troyna and Williams 1986). The confusion about terms is inevitable. Educators' responses are what are essential to equity and diversity education: that is, the feelings, the behaviour, and the beliefs that are evoked by the deliberate intention to correct inequities in the system.

Third, equity and diversity education expresses our desire to overcome internecine conflicts among ideological camps of equity advocates, conflicts that jeopardize nascent alliances. We believe that those internal struggles for a rightful place in the arena of policy development divert energy from the achievement of what are ultimately shared goals.

RESPONSES TO EQUITY
AND DIVERSITY EDUCATION

How have efforts to integrate equity and diversity education fared? Educational projects intended to effectively address racial and other forms of inequities have met with tenacious resistance. Resistance is a term that has been used in more than one way in the sociology of education. Since the publication of Paul Willis' classic *Learning to Labour* (1977), the term has been used to describe the constructive, politically insightful movement of a subordinate social group against the forces operating to reproduce and maintain its subordinate status in an essentially inequitable society.[2] In Willis' study, a group of under-achieving young men sustain a resistance to conform to an educational system aimed at working-class youth bound for working-class jobs. Their culture is studied up close and Willis interprets the "lads'" defiant behaviour as a creative response to the structures that work to control them and assign them an inferior social status.

As popular as this notion of resistance has become, particularly among advocates of critical pedagogy, our usage of "resistance" is different. Perhaps it may be regarded as more traditional in meaning. In our usage, resistance is a political act exercised by groups with authority who are struggling against pressure to change their social interactions. The definitive feature of this resistance is the intransigent conservative ideologies and practices that underpin the response.

Resistance indicates a (conservative) oppositional stance that is manifest in a variety of ways. It thus shares some of the qualities of the productive yet paradoxical resistance observed in subordinate groups (Giroux 1983; Jackson 1999; Solomon 1992; Willis 1977), but is actually closer to the more parochial meaning found in Bagley (1992), James (1995b), Mansfield and Kehoe (1994), Ouseley (1992) and others. Here, it describes the actions not of a subordinate group that resists efforts to control it, but of a group that occupies a position of power within the context of a formal organization. Resistance of school agents is expressed from a location of political conservatism, and its target is progressive educational change. It communicates opposition to the challenge to the status quo equity and diversity education implies.

Conversely, we use the term "accommodation" to identify not a grudging compromise (although this can accompany the response) but any form of positive response to and implementation of equity and diversity education regardless of its consequences. It indicates an adoption of some, usually outward, aspects of equity and diversity education such as specific curricular projects. Signs of a deeper change to the underlying structures or ideologies informing the way teaching operates is generally absent. Resistance and accommodation may be manifest in teachers' actions, beliefs, feelings, or combinations of these. Their expectations, intentions, and beliefs about personal responses vary widely among these participants.

Practitioners and theorists alike have vigorously challenged the way educators have conceptualized and implemented equity educational reforms. In this book we argue that multicultural and anti-racism pedagogy has been slow in achieving the objective of equalizing opportunities for racial and ethnic minorities because of educators' ambivalence, contradictory responses, or outright antagonism to its concept, policy and practice. Such responses are well documented in the literature (Donaldson 2001; Levine-Rasky 2000a; Nieto 1995; Troyna 1993).

In Britain, for instance, the introduction of anti-racism in the 1980s was criticized by mainstream educators for imposing the salience of race on a previously neutral, "colour-blind" educational system and for exploiting education as a means of indoctrination. From this conservative perspective, anti-racism is perceived to be confrontational, radical, and antithetical to the more harmonious, benevolent multiculturalism (Honeyford 1986; Jeffcoate 1984; Short and Carrington 1996). According to Ben-Tovim, Gabriel, Law and Stredder (1991, 206) raising the question of race and racism in a society that professes to be colour-blind is perceived as "divisive, an incitement to racial discord or an invitation to 'white backlash.'" Further, teacher autonomy, they argue, would be severely restricted in a classroom environment that ought to be "neutral" and unencumbered by the kind of ideology that detractors believe is attached to equity and diversity education.

In Canada, critics have continued to marginalize ethnocultural equity and anti-racism utilizing similar arguments to those of their British counterparts. Research on personal and institutional responses to race and ethnocultural issues in education reveal "... there is often tremendous resistance to overcome in policy development and implementation; this resistance may be obvious or covert" (Mock and Masemann 1990, 59). Mansfield and Kehoe cite what they perceive to be conceptual, empirical, and political limitations of anti-racist education and conclude that such interventions "show negligible and even negative results" (1994, 418).

Teacher resistance to innovation and change has been receiving notice in the sociology of education literature. Acker (1988) argues that teacher resistance to new initiatives, especially those concerning equity, may be the result of a number of factors. The nature of the initiative itself may be perceived to be an imposition, threatening, and/or counterproductive to other programs.

The conditions of work encompassing the micropolitics of the school, the general level of support for educational reform found in the overall climate in the school, and the nature of teachers' expanding role may influence reluctance to change. Characteristics of teachers such as their age, race and ethnicity, social class, and degree of conservatism may also affect receptivity to reform. Finally, teachers' ideologies, norms, values, traditions, beliefs, and assumptions may influence their positions, attitudes, and behaviours toward any initiative that disturbs traditional approaches. According to Corbett, Firestone and Rossman (1987), the likelihood of a positive or negative response to change depends on the fit between the proposed change and the culture of the school. "Change is greeted with suspicion and reluctance," say the authors, "when expectations for behavior embedded in a new practice, policy or program do not coincide with existing conceptions of the way school life is or should be" (36).

RESEARCH APPROACHES

The study on which Part I of this book is based is from a large research project conducted in Canada in the early to mid-1990s. It is informed by the work of researchers around the world, which has demonstrated that there is a poor translation from statements on equity and diversity education to amelioration of educational outcomes for all groups of students. Educators have not embraced equity and diversity education; accommodation has been piecemeal or superficial. Most studies concerned with why this may be so are speculative and have neglected to solicit teachers' perspectives directly. In addition, most have been restricted to local jurisdictions. Studies on a national scale are rare.

In an effort to fill this gap in our understanding of teachers' perspectives on equity and diversity education, our study for Part I of this book was designed on a large scale and sought subjective accounts from participants. It utilized both quantitative (survey) and qualitative (interview) approaches, as well as archival material in the data collection process. School board selection for this study was based on the presence of racial and ethnocultural diversity in their student populations and the existence of a formal multicultural and/or anti-racist (race relations) education policy. On this basis, five urban centres were selected from the provinces of British Columbia, Manitoba, Nova Scotia and Ontario. Documents describing educational policies on equity and diversity were collected for each of these provinces and the respective urban centres where the research was conducted.

The survey, distributed only to teachers, contained three sections. The first elicited respondents' demographic and background characteristics such as sex, ethnicity, years of teaching experience and school panel (see Table 1.1). The second section consisted of 55 statements, utilizing a 5-point Likert response scale to ascertain teacher perspectives on various aspects of multicultural and anti-racist education policy and practice. Survey items covered the following themes: those pertaining to goals; policy; teaching practices (classroom strategies); community relations; other school practices; specific beliefs about pedagogy; general beliefs about race, ethnicity, and racism; beliefs about multicultural and anti-racist education; professional development for diversity; and other related professional issues and personal evaluations. The third section of the survey solicited additional comments in an unstructured manner and requested volunteers for follow-up interviews.

For this multi-site study, co-investigators with research skills and knowledge of the professional territory were employed to distribute, conduct, and collect the survey, to do a preliminary analysis of the survey data, and to conduct the follow-up interviews. Teachers completed 1,002 surveys and 227 additional information sheets in 57 elementary and secondary schools from the five school jurisdictions across Canada. Follow-up interviews were designed to probe for more detail as well as the meanings behind attitudes, beliefs, and practices.

Three groups of educators were interviewed: 35 teachers who participated in the survey, 10 school administrators (principals and vice-principals), and six multicultural/anti-racist education advisors[3] employed by school boards. Purposive sampling of participants for interviews ensured a balanced representation of sex, years of teaching experience, and grade level and subjects taught. Two administrators from each participating school board (one elementary and one secondary) and the multicultural/anti-racist education advisor assigned to each of the five Boards of Education were interviewed. (In one school jurisdiction there are two advisors, accounting for the total of six). While teachers were able to volunteer for the interview, the other participants were solicited directly.

The demographic profile of interview respondents reflects that of the survey respondents in racial identity, gender, teaching panel, and length of teaching experience (see Table 1.1). Of the 35 classroom teachers interviewed, 32 were of European-Canadian heritage, while 2 were of African-Canadian and 1 of Asian-Canadian heritage. All 10 school administrators were of the dominant European group. However, there was much more racial balance in the advisors' group: 3 were African-Canadian, 2 European-Canadian, and 1

Asian-Canadian. Just over half of the 35 classroom teachers were females, while 75% of the school administrators and MCE/ARE advisors were male. Those educators (classroom teachers and administrators) working in the elementary panel (grades 1 to 8) comprised slightly over half of the respondents (24 of 45), while there was a balanced representation of teachers in years of experience. In the presentation of interview data, respondents will be identified by school board and respondents' status as teachers, school administrators, or advisors; other identifying data will be used where appropriate.[4]

Data collection and analysis followed a process that Glaser and Strauss (1967), Erickson (1986), and LeCompte and Preissle (1993) describe as the constant comparison method. The initial survey was followed by a preliminary analysis of the data. This analysis provided frequencies and cross tabulations that indicated patterns for further exploration. Important themes for further investigation also emerged from the additional comments attached to the survey questionnaires. From these data sources, separate follow-up interview protocols were generated for teachers, school administrators and MCE/ARE advisors. Interviews were audiotaped and transcribed verbatim for coding and analysis. From these, broad categories were generated to represent the data before reducing them to specific emergent themes.

The findings that follow are based on the analysis of both the survey and interview data, but are more firmly grounded in the interviews. These interviews probed for the determinants and implications of the attitudes, beliefs, and practices that emerged from survey responses. This qualitative approach was emphasized because it allowed a deeper and more complex exploration of participants' beliefs necessary in an inquiry as emotionally charged and sensitive as this one.

In keeping with the qualitative research tradition, this book locates the problem of tensions in teacher responses to equity and diversity education, opting for an elaboration of the nature of the responses and the patterns they presented. This position should be regarded as a balance between offering meaningful explanations of teachers' aggregate responses to equity and diversity education and the significance of the lived experience of particular social actors. Rather than suggesting a uniform process of data analysis, it thus carries on in the style of debates in educational research in which questions about a particular approach are not answered as often as they are integrated, interpreted, and negotiated (see for example LeCompte and Preissle 1993).

The Urban Diversity Teacher Education Program at York University in Ontario (Canada) largely informs the second part of this book which is divided into four chapters. Chapter 5: *Racial Identity Development and Teaching*, explores the conception of racial identity and examines how attitudes, beliefs,

Table 1.1
Survey Respondents' School Board, Gender, Ethnicity, Years of Teaching experience and Teaching Panel

Major Category	Sub-Category	N	%
School Board	Board 1: Nova Scotia	203	20.3
	Board 2: Ontario	258	25.7
	Board 3: Ontario	258	25.7
	Board 4: Manitoba	139	13.9
	Board 5: British Columbia	144	14.4
		Total 1002	100.0
Gender	Female	561	56.0
	Male	328	32.7
	Not Given	113	11.3
		Total 1002	100.0
Ethnicity	Canadian*	330	32.9
	European British	287	28.6
	European Continental	226	22.6
	Racial Minority	81	8.1
	Other	20	2.0
	No Ethnic Identification	58	5.8
		Total 1002	100.0
Years of Teaching Experience	0-5	187	19.4
	6-10	122	12.7
	11-15	113	11.7
	16-20	195	20.2
	21-25	169	17.5
	26+	178	18.5
		Total 964	100.0
School Panel	Elementary	498	49.7
	Secondary	504	50.3
		Total 1002	100.0

* While the survey asked respondents to self-identify in terms of "heritage/ethnicity," 32.9% chose to describe themselves only as "Canadian." See Appendix A, Endnote 1 for an elaboration.

perceptions, worldviews, and knowledge may develop in persons who are necessarily "racialized" within a "racialized" social and political environment.

Chapter 6: *Cross-Race Dyad Partnerships in Pre-service Teacher Education*, is based on the rationale that teachers' cross-race collaboration during the process of learning to teach will help to break down racial barriers, tackle sensitive racial and cultural issues, and provide models of inter-group collaboration. The model for the study employed in this chapter is an approach that twins a teacher from the dominant racial background and a teacher from a minority racial background and provides them an extended opportunity to develop both their teaching skills and professional relationships in a collaborative and interdependent manner.

Chapter 7: *Community Involvement: A Service Learning Approach to Teacher Education*, outlines the issues, advantages, and praxis of the service learning approach to teacher education. This model builds upon the educational philosopher and practitioner John Dewey's belief that progressive education entails the active and constructive involvement of teachers within the communities in which they work. The service learning approach here is undertaken to counteract the lack of direct experience that dominant group educators are likely to have with the minority communities within which they are called upon to teach. Chapter 8: *The Professional Development School as a "Community of Learners"* outlines the importance of developing a "culture" whereby specific schools become teacher education sites within which veteran and new teacher candidates can share their knowledge and experiences in a school-university collaborative project. Together, the chapters that comprise Part II of this book incorporate and structurally examine the integral theoretical and practical constituents of what can be an effective anti-racist teacher education program.

ENDNOTES

1. In this book, the indigenous peoples of North America are labeled variously and interchangeably by our research respondents and the research literature as Aboriginal peoples, Natives, Native Indians, American Indians, and First Nations or Aboriginal peoples (the latter —First Nations—almost exclusively a Canadian designation).

2. This meaning of "resistance" is also rooted in another classic text, yet one that describes a completely different social environment than that of Willis' lads. Eugene Genovese's (1972) *Roll Jordan, Roll: The World the Slaves Made* is an epic in social historical research detailing the American slave culture that emerged from the struggle for dignity under the system of chattel slavery. This text extinguishes the myth of the acquiescent black slave.

3. At the time of field research, advisors were variously designated Race Relations Advisor, Multiculturalism Consultant, Equity Advisor, etc. by their school board employer. These labels also evolved over time. To maintain consistency in this book we have used the designation Advisor or MCE/ARE advisor throughout.

Teaching for Equity and Diversity

4. Interview respondents are coded by school board or region of origin (R), and their status within their regions; for example, teacher (T), principal or vice principal elementary (PE), principal/vice principal secondary (PS), MCE/ARE advisor (A). In addition, teachers were coded T1 to T7 and advisors A, A1 or A2 to differentiate among them. Examples of coding:

> R1T4: Region 1, Teacher 4
> R3PE: Region 3, Principal Elementary
> R4PS: Region 4, Principal Secondary
> R5A2: Region 5, Advisor 2

chapter two

Racism, Ethnocentrism, and Educational Inequity

Meanings of equity and diversity are conferred through an act of interpretation. This chapter explores teachers' subjective interpretations of what constitutes difference, racism and ethnocentrism, and educational inequity. The system of meanings, representations, and values embedded in concrete practices structure teachers' subjectivity and underlie the sense of meaning they bring to activities. Educators are not determined products of a regulated socialization process that blindly subscribe to educational theory or to the inherited conditions of teaching. They are active participants in the culture of the school, and the knowledge they encounter is interpreted and evaluated, accommodated and absorbed, reflected and reacted upon according to their personal version of what is true and meaningful.

Responses are contingent upon establishing a close fit with a personal interpretive framework and its associated values and investments. These positions inform, in turn, the sense an educator makes of difference and educational inequality as it impacts upon the lives of marginalized groups. They also inform how an educator implements equity and diversity education and the degree to which it will be accommodated or resisted.

THE MEANING OF DIFFERENCE

For our participants, racial and ethnic identity are often thoroughly integrated with notions of an essential difference. Concurrent reflections on the norm from which others are believed to deviate are rare. There is superficial understanding about the nationality we all share as North Americans or about multiple cultural identities. What consequences are created when notions of "Canadian" or "American" exclude those groups who, by virtue of their outward appearance or first-language usage, are designated as "different"? These categories intimate a value judgment tempered with a self-consciousness that may reflect participants' internal conflicts. Some educators unselfconsciously understand the category "Canadian" to mean "white" or an individual or group descending from a European heritage, as in these excerpts from interviews with teachers:

> He looks like your stereotype (Sikh) but when he talks he's a real Canadian. But he doesn't look your average Canadian... yet he has this turban on and he's very affable, gregarious. (R5T5)

> Most of my students are Canadians and most of them are originally from here; the kids are from this country. There is just one girl who is a mix between a Canadian mother and a father with a Caribbean [background]. (R3T3)

In this last excerpt, the teacher confirms that this child is Canadian-born. The perspective on what constitutes "us" as firmly distinct from "them" provokes many questions. What criteria are required for children to be counted as Canadian? What is the consequence of being permanently excluded from sharing a nationality? What of safeguarding the inclusion of new immigrants? While more vulnerable, immigrants' membership in Canadian society is, after all, their right to claim.

If racial or ethnic minorities are situated outside the cultural borders that define Canadian society, what is the nature of that norm? One school principal reveals the presumed neutrality of the Canadian norm that affects and is derived from race and class distinctions even while erasing those distinctions:

> From a racial mix [this school] is probably culturally sterile. I would call it culturally sterile... . People keep pretty much to themselves and everybody has the same general type of values and they're straight middle class values. (R1PE)

For this administrator, to be Caucasian and middle class is to have no culture, nothing upon which to reflect. Further, middle class values are established as seamless and unified, the meaning of which can be taken for granted. This set of assumptions constructs neutral strata. More complex approaches to cultural identity are rendered as deviations.

Some interview participants commonly articulate stereotypes of racial and ethnic minorities. Generalizations about the academic "inferiority of Blacks" or their "lack of pride" and the educational "superiority" of various Asian groups were made. With respect to our survey item, "Student commitment to education varies across racial/ethnic groups," a full 55.8% of educators agreed, 26.2% disagreed, and 15.6% remained ambivalent. This indicates a relatively common belief that academic performance is correlated with students' membership in a racial or ethnic group.

Specific remarks about groups were often made self-consciously or were corrected or qualified after their first mention. It is possible that educators are currently engaged in integrating contemporary ideas about social difference or in developing sensitivity about the experiences of others, or perhaps they were merely indicating their concern to appear "politically correct" in the interview.

More research would have to be conducted to fully explain the cautious and sometimes painful self-consciousness with which these remarks were made:

> They're not all Africans. And by African I mean 'Negroid?' If you wonder what I mean, because some of them don't want to be called 'Blacks' and there's no such thing as the 'Black' race and all this sort of business that's been in the air. (R2T5)

> So they're good students, they're hardworking students, you know, I'm generalizing of course and there are going to be some who aren't, but by and large they're nice kids to work with. My goodness, was that a racist comment—I'm generalizing aren't I? All the kids at [this school] are good kids, well I'm generalizing again, there are a few that I can think of. (R4T4)

"Colour-blindness" is another common response to teaching in environments of racial and ethnic diversity (Chatter 1996; Cochran-Smith 1995; McLaren and Torres 1999; Schofield 1997). In allowing a teacher to sidestep the acknowledgement of difference, this presents a dilemma. The desire to be sensitive to particular racial and ethnic identities vies with the desire to treat all children as though they were the same. Moreover, "colour-blindness" effectively discounts racial and ethnic difference that distinguishes individuals from each other. How do the teachers express this tension? Some examples follow:

> I won't forget that you come from a different culture and have different values, different expectations, and different background. I'll treat you

all the same... . I see the individual first and then put the individual into context of what I would know of their culture and experience. (R5T7)

I think some people use colour-blind as an excuse for like, "Well, I don't treat them any differently so I don't have to worry about it," but then there is a good aspect of it too. If you do see them so totally as individuals that it doesn't become a salient feature about the child and maybe that's what some people mean when they think of it as colour-blind. (R3T2)

Even in a case in which the teacher discusses skin colour openly, the meanings students themselves make of the issue are neglected:

They all were interested to pick up their exact skin tone to put on their pictures. That's probably one of the few times when we kind of dealt with the thing directly because we talked about white and black and I showed them what white paint and black paint and white paper and black paper [look like] and I had children come up and compare their skin [to these colours to show] that nobody is white or black and some people who racially are African their skin might be lighter in fact than some of the children who were "white." (R3T2)

Table 2.1 illustrates the frequency of responses to colour-blindness and to a related emphasis on homogeneity in the classroom in such a way that a contradiction is revealed. If one professes colour-blindness, then presumably one would emphasize similarity and suppress difference in the classroom. Yet this does not necessarily follow. Many educators describe themselves as colour-blind but they are evenly divided when asked to evaluate anti-racism in terms of the way difference is stressed.

Some teachers express colour-blindness without concern for how children's racial or ethnic heritage may be of significance. This naïveté increases a teacher's distance from her students as in the following excerpt:

In about February I deal with the Native People and the Voyageurs and that sort of thing [in the curriculum] and when that comes up I have many, many children raise their hand and say, "I'm part Indian," and you wouldn't know to look at them at all. (R4T4)

Later she adds that religious difference is too private a topic for discussion,

Teaching for Equity and Diversity

Table 2.1
Teachers' Responses to Social Difference and Anti-racist Education

Valid percent

Item	Agree/ Strongly Agree	Disagree/ Strongly Disagree	Ambivalent	n
I am colour-blind when it comes to working with students of diverse racial groups.	63.2	19.6	12.4	959
ARE over-emphasizes student differences at the expense of their similarities.	29.6	37.1	30.3	971

preventing her awareness of religious difference among her students. For other educators, the disregard for social difference seems to be a convenient way to legitimate their own politically conservative theories about teaching and social difference.

Ironically, the enactment of these theories may produce the very inequities in groups of children that colour-blindness is intended to alleviate. Indeed, the erasure of difference plays a central part in some personal theories about what is important in human interaction. One highly experienced white teacher speaks proudly of his colour-blindness—which he feels he developed following many years of feeling "hyper-aware" of racial difference. His story is revealing in many ways:

> When I moved here, when I saw the African population increase, I started to wonder, "Am I prejudiced?" Do I carry all these prejudices? And for quite a few years I was going around being hyper-aware of, you know, "Am I prejudiced?" "Am I prejudiced?" "Oh, there's a group of black students." Now, I have to keep very much aware that they're black, and pretend that I'm just acting normal as if they're normal people. And I had to go through that getting used to it. And now I think I can honestly say that I don't see people by their colour any more. I don't notice that. (R2T5)

What is the net effect of this teacher's colour-blindness? Is it a complete rejection of practices that demonstrate a differentiation between groups? Is it an increased sensitivity to the lives of others, to their stories of resistance and complicity with dominant versions of what is valued or rewarded?

We would expect colour-blindness to lead to an improved participation in classroom activities. Unfortunately, such expectations are dashed. In the remainder of his interview, this teacher demonstrates that he derives satisfaction from confirming his belief that "people are people" only when their histories are rendered irrelevant and their willingness to assimilate to the eurocentric "Canadian" norm is established. In his classes, the vehicle of international literature serves the purpose of "proving" the existence of a universal human nature that legitimates an unexamined white, male, middle class image of the very definition of personhood. Racial difference is regarded as absolute, distinct from a national identity, which all citizens may rightfully claim.

Upon examination, colour-blindness, while ostensibly a channel for rectifying educational inequity on the basis of race, guarantees no such commitment. In fact, it often conceals a teacher's interest in perpetuating educational inequity through an expectation for students to assimilate. Concurrently, racism, ethnocentrism, and educational inequity are generally deflected to interactions that take place beyond the purview of one's classroom or school if they are acknowledged at all. In this conservative view, personal territory is defended and equity and diversity education is interpreted as a threat to the way social relations are justly organized.

In a discussion of white teachers' conceptualizations of race and educational inequity, Sleeter (1993) explains that colour-blindness is a myth that Whites use to suppress their negative images of racial minorities. Realizing the safety in behaving as though race and ethnicity were of no significance in schooling, teachers are motivated to avoid questions that force the designation of group (or individual) racial or ethnic identity. Since equity and diversity education embraces such questions, teachers' resistance to it is a result.

Running parallel to a rejection of equity and diversity education is the unwillingness to discuss educational inequity as a problem that follows the contours of a racial and ethnic difference. Through the use of alternative or "coded" terms, teachers may "explain away the subordination of people of colour" (Sleeter 1993, 168). The currency of terms such as "high-risk," "under-achievement," "urban poor," "inner-city," and "low status" function as outlets for the identification and rationalization of racial and ethnic minorities' social inequality (Banks 2001; Dei and Calliste 2000; Fine 1991). Troyna (1994) speaks of this as a process of de-racialization, in which what is essentially a problem of race relations becomes translated into a more benign and thus more manageable problem of others' inadequacies.

Difference is an erasable feature of social identity for some teachers because it insults their sense that their primary function is to assimilate students to the "Canadian" way of life. Here is one excerpt that illustrates this orientation:

> I think it's [MCE/ARE] basically trying to bring these new Canadians into the mainstream, into the group, helping them to adapt to a new culture. Making them feel accepted at home, part of the group. I think that's probably the number one thing as far as education that we probably should be doing. Making them—not only the children but their parents as well—aware of our society and how things work and how they can live in it. (R3T1)

The belief in the assimilation of racial and ethnic minorities into the dominant Canadian culture, despite the country's 1971 and 1988 policies on multiculturalism, is exemplified in this interview excerpt:

> Sometimes too much emphasis is placed on minority groups and they expect too much from society. There may be little adjustment required of the minority group to adapt and adjust to society as a whole and the ways of society to help to keep it uniformed (sic). (R1T1)

Suppressing social difference so as to enforce assimilation to the white, European, middle class norm is evident in the comments of many teachers. This political view lies behind the belief that ethnicity will decline in significance over time as ethnically defined groups achieve economic success (Greenman, Kimmel, Bannan and Radford-Curry 1992; Sleeter, 1993).

White ethnic immigrants can become structurally assimilated into the dominant society despite initial social class and language barriers (Alba 1999; Omi and Winant 1994). Visibly identifiable racial minorities such as Blacks and Native peoples, however, face many additional obstacles that restrict their status to the lower ranks of the socio-economic system.

In Canada, the history of racial and ethnic differences in socio-economic system and mobility patterns is well documented (Agocs and Jain 2001; Kalbach and Kalbach 1999; Li 1988; Pendakur 1996). Structural inequities faced by racial minority groups make it extremely difficult for them to "make it" in the mainstream culture compared to members of groups of European heritage (Stelcner and Kyriazis 1995; Walker 1987; Winks 1971).

This position carries some similarity to that of a teacher who believes that racial and ethnic identity is integral to a Canadian identity:

We are different and you're allowed to be different and you're encouraged to be different. Because of our multicultural fabric, elements of racism converge because of impact, really.... We're all immigrants. We just came earlier; some earlier and some later. (R5T7)

The problem here lies in the disregard for the particular conditions that attend the integration of racial and minority groups. Their inclusion into mainstream society has been, and continues to be, met with profound structural and cultural barriers.

Yet, for some, the very mention of social difference qualifies as an offense. In one unsolicited additional comment on the survey, one respondent represents this view that he expresses emphatically: "Kids are Kids. Help them be the best whatever they can be" (R2T1). This popular position ignores questions a critic may raise such as: Who decides what is "the best?" Who evaluates the potential of a child? Who is given the power to facilitate that potential?

A related view based on conservative politics is the reification of a uniform, singular national identity. Upon inspection, definitions of membership do not include all citizens but only those who share a common, European heritage. One teacher, for example, insists, "[t]his country was founded by Native Peoples and people of British North American descent. You can't ignore this fact because you are trying to be politically correct... " (R3T7)

Others evoke the concept of the "pure Canadian" in their argument as though this image were an historical and social fact. The construction focuses not only upon the exclusion or inclusion of "Canadian" forms, but communicates a positive relative value to the dominant culture, relegating that of "others" to a lesser value. It seeks to diminish the input, the history, the stories, the struggles, and the lived cultural experiences of a large and integral proportion of Canadians. In addition, it assigns members of minority groups ultimate responsibility for what some educators perceive to be their unwillingness or inability to assimilate to the "Canadian" way of life, an ironic position when read from the point of view of those excluded from participating in those mainstream activities.

One revealing example selected from a survey participant's written comments is presented here:

Multicultural education is wonderful, but we have forgotten something very basic. Our job is to teach or orientate new Canadians to the Canadian way or history or culture, whatever you call it. If we only cater to MCE we are doing our children a disservice. The Canadian way is to negotiate, live together, talk—work things out. We *do* have some traditions; let us celebrate some *Canadianisms*. We have gone a little too far with MCE. (R3T7)

For those teachers interested in demarcating a "Canadian" identity, teaching from an equity and diversity perspective may imply the exclusion of the dominant group. This perspective represents an extreme form of resistance to equity and diversity education:

I don't have any other reason [for resistance to equity and diversity education] except that we shouldn't just recognize one group. We should recognize everybody and teach their background. Why just one group? Here we're trying to have everybody getting along together and here we're recognizing one group. I mean, why not have white Canada month or something? (R2T2)

Somehow, the disturbing messages embedded in the above remarks are unaffected by reassurances by some educators, that "white groups need not feel alienated because bringing other cultures into the classroom or society does not mean throwing out the white culture" (R2T6). The politically conservative remarks allude to the preservation of a particular set of cultural forms and the control over their dispensation. Other concerns, such as the study of different cultural forms, are preempted in this agenda. The justice of sharing control over public education with racial and ethnic communities is suppressed.

Responses to equity and diversity education may involve a backlash that works to justify the latent fears of members of dominant groups. One teacher writes, "Reverse discrimination is much more evident with students [who are] taking 'empowerment' to the point of defiance and challenge." (R2T5) This teacher does not appreciate the situation as it has existed in historical race relations. Somehow the morality of white "defiance and challenge" to the objectives of equity and diversity education escapes his notice.

For another white teacher, this position has developed into a well-honed argument. Racism, for him, is a matter of an intransigent black community "holding a grudge" about past injustices. "White superiority," this teacher argues, "is an issue that Blacks or African-heritage people are carrying around with them." (R2T5) He blames the group itself for mounting a barrier to alleviating the very problem it is "complaining" about. Racism is an imagined construction, and its effects are played out among student groups rather than in student-teacher or student-institution interactions. For this teacher, racism is a myth perpetuated by the hostility of disenfranchised and misguided youth who target innocent educators such as himself as their current "victim" (R2T5).

This politically conservative perspective is intended to preserve the hegemony and presumed entitlement of the dominant cultural group. Challenges to the monolithic "Canadian" culture provoke what Roman (1993) calls "white defensiveness," in which people of European heritage reverse roles with historically oppressed groups. They claim the position of victim on this basis. Beverly Gordon (1985) explains:

> While steeped in our common sense notions of humanism, equity, and parity, we are faced with the sticky dilemma of attempting to educate the masses in a way that allows them accessibility to high status knowledge and places them on an equal footing to compete. Most assuredly in time, they will compete with our children and ostensibly with us for a share of the power and the reallocation of resources. And while most people do have good intentions, when our social status is threatened, we tend to become even more conservative in order to protect our material gains. (37)

INTERPRETATIONS OF RACISM AND ETHNOCENTRISM

There is little hope that equity and diversity education will be supported if the existence of racism and ethnocentrism is denied. Yet this finding is widespread in our as well as others' research (Dei and Karumanchery, 2001; Foster 1990; King 1991; Troyna 1993). Although 58.5% of survey respondents disagreed that racism is not evident at their school, 19.4% agreed, and 18.8% were ambivalent.

Supportive administrators and advisors speak of teachers' scant awareness of the social issues attached to an equity and diversity imperative. They note the denial of any problem in the area of racism, ethnocentrism, educational equity, or differential treatment and experiences of students. They see a widespread denial of social inequality:

> I think the big thing is they have not dealt with it themselves. They have not really looked at their thoughts and beliefs... . Like everything is great. "It doesn't affect me. I'm white, I'm middle-class, I've got a job. I'm fine and everybody else in the world is fine." Just because you

haven't dealt with abuse and oppression doesn't mean that the person next door hasn't experienced it; and that's where a lot of people feel that it doesn't exist. (R1T3)

One race relation's advisor (R5A2) gives contradictory reports about denial, but finally expresses his frustration with "the slow pace of implementation and the denial that continues to persist." According to this advisor, resistance is mainly manifest in educators' lack of commitment to equity and diversity. Blatant and disturbing incidents (in the classroom) of a racist or ethnocentric nature are typically regarded as a problem restricted to the individuals involved. Racism and ethnocentrism is someone else's problem. For reasons of social propriety and the personal implications it engenders, racial or ethnic difference has been a topic that escapes articulation for members of dominant groups. The naming of difference and, concomitantly, racism or ethnocentrism is often deflected to other phenomena that are easier for speakers to utter.

In the following coded narratives, the malevolence of racism becomes attributed to more benign social interactions:

I wouldn't think it has anything to do with race. I think it's just part of human relationships; learning to get along with each other and respect for each other's feelings. Basically we're all the same and I think that's what kids have to learn. (R2T5)

I guess racism is another aspect of human nature. (R2T2)

Various educators in ways that obviate the deeper analysis necessary for their elimination often mis-define racism and ethnocentrism. Racism is often only counted as such when it is manifested in overt activities such as physical or verbal attacks. Name-calling and inappropriate epithets for groups are commonplace. Yet even in these cases, some educators are not necessarily moved to advocate or implement a systematic program for the eradication of racism:

The worst graffiti we had was around the time of the multicultural activities. Like the KKKs [Klu Klux Klans] appeared quite a bit during the time because they react.... The person will just take his black marker and write a big KKK on things that involved minority people.... Last year I spent a lot of time erasing KKKs. (R1T2)

One teacher responded to name-calling by a Chilean, a Chinese, and a student of both African and European heritage in the following way:

> I said, "Put your arms together, and let's have a look at this arm and this arm and this arm." We got the three arms together. "What colour is that?" Oh, they couldn't tell me what colour it was. They're all about the same, and one's calling the other a different colour. You couldn't tell the difference in their arms. (R5T5)

Even when involving European-Canadian students, racism is limited to hostility among students alone:

> Maybe the area they come from is predominantly White, but when they come to Canada, all of a sudden they're forced to blend or mix with other minority groups, and having to deal with it. The parents first of all don't know how to deal with it and therefore the kids aren't equipped to deal with it. Sometimes the kids come in with the attitude that a non-white is totally below a white person and they have no qualms about showing it. (R3T7)

The elimination of discrimination and racism presupposes their acknowledgement. The problem is that they are interpreted in ways that prohibit acknowledgement. Educators, like many others, attribute these problems to a range of factors quite divorced from their own scope of activity.

If racism and ethnocentrism are something "out there" "among them" or caused by factors beyond one's control, the individual is absolved from initiating change. Usually no conscious connections are made between observed racism and ethnocentrism, and resistance to educational programs that could draw attention to covert patterns of educational inequality. Teachers resist the conclusion that the way they regard social difference perpetuates racism or may even qualify as racism itself. While many educators increasingly embrace the principle of diversity, the social problems that attend it are not examined in a light that would effectively explain their persistence.

There is some acknowledgement that racism exists in subtle forms. Here, a teacher describes how marginalization is exercised by teachers or by school procedures, respectively:

> There might be unconscious ways that you might be like choosing the white, blond-haired children to stand all the time at the front of the line

may seem like a simple thing, but it may be the kind of thing that gives the class the impression that they're [white kids] superior because they're always going first so that's so subtle and you don't realize you're doing it... . And you do things without thinking. Habits are done without thinking. So yes, it goes on. It's not overt, it's not malicious, it's not deliberate. It's an unconscious habit. (R2T6)

Speaking of teachers' behaviour, one participant states that racism "does not necessarily manifest itself in racial slurs or name-calling. But it comes up in other things" (R1T3). If racism is denied to exist "directly," to mention one remark, then it could still be regarded as indirectly guiding social interactions and school policies and practices (R2T6). One administrator says explicitly with regard to making racist generalizations about Blacks:

I do it and I'm not going to sit and say that I don't do it. I mean I can be as subtle as the next person. We know when to dish it in and out if we had to. (R1PE)

Others understand racism as a pervasive quality of our Canadian society:

We live in a racist culture. I mean, we all do; the teachers, everybody. I get really upset when I hear teachers in this holier-than-thou attitude that "I'm not a racist." Unless you grow up on a desert island, you are a racist, a sexist, you're a homophobic, quite likely. (R1T3)

A school administrator states:

Anybody who tells me there's no racism in their school is full of you know what... . I don't buy for two minutes that there's not racism in our school. To me that's nonsense just given the nature of society. (R4PE)

Racism, while it may not be called that directly, is noted among teachers who are themselves members of racial and ethnic minorities. One African-Canadian teacher draws upon her personal experience as a parent and suggests that "black students are penalized for being promoted too quickly... . Black students are not expected to achieve academically and the teacher is not happy with a black child who is in an advanced placement" (R1T5).

Others describe racism and ethnocentrism from the point of view of an insider:

It's in you. I'm an immigrant, you see. And when I came over I suffered racial prejudice in many ways. There are many situations where people don't think anything but the way they look at you, and then they talk to you like you don't know how to speak English. And it hurts. (R4T7)

My own children are visible minorities and they're asked where were they born and they say, "Excuse me... what do you mean? I was born in [the local] hospital." You know, they'll play with it and they'll refuse to answer. And that exposes their own assumption that "I'm different" until they can force a breakdown to "Oh, I see, you looked at me and thought I was different so you assumed I couldn't be born here. Interesting." (R5T7)

Yet some teachers needn't identify with marginalization personally to declare that some of their colleagues are racist:

One student I had was in an English class and the teacher tried so hard to get her to take the General level. And she kept asking her really to leave her Advanced[1] class... . The girl was insistent and never did leave and she did well in the course eventually. And I would say that this particular teacher would always encourage students from certain cultures to take the General level courses. (R3T6)

While racism may not always be denied in the schools, its full appreciation is not carried to its logical end. Change is blocked as long as educators themselves are naive in recognizing their participation in exclusionary practices in ways as innocent as this:

How does racism manifest itself? You see, I don't understand it. You know, I don't really understand racism because I, you know I don't feel like I am racist. Maybe, maybe I am; I don't feel I am, so I don't know how it manifests itself in the classes. (R5T3)

A secondary school teacher tells of the risk and multiple meanings of becoming more aware of the possibility of racism in classroom interactions:

I certainly think it's something people do have to be aware of. You know, are you dealing fairly with this student? Are you taking the perspective that they're a different culture and dealing with them differently?... You didn't think about the fact that they had a different colour skin. I mean, that didn't enter your mind at all, but we are aware of it because we are aware that there is the potential of someone saying to you, "Are you doing that because you feel some kind of racism?" "No, I wasn't, I would do that to any student." You know, you've got to really pay attention to being fair or it could come out looking like you, you know, aren't fair and you are racist. (R5T3)

As this teacher describes the consequences of making unconscious differentiations in her treatment of schoolchildren, she is faced with the inadequacy of "colour-blindness." Her motivation about acknowledging racism is purely utilitarian, however, serving to protect teachers' professional status rather than to promote a moral sensibility.

ON EDUCATIONAL INEQUITIES

Some educators deny that the educational system is inequitable for some groups of students. An example follows:

English level will certainly affect them. But not colour and not race and not sex, not gender... . You tend to just mark. I mean, a math test is a math test. If the thing adds up to 45 out of 45, you cannot change the mark. I strongly disagree with that. I don't think people teach differently. And [with respect to] the argument of streaming black kids into sports, I don't see that either. Because there are klutzes in that race. There are klutzes in every race. I strongly disagree with that. I have never seen it after 12 years. (R2T1)

According to this teacher, student achievement follows no collective pattern. There are only individuals' behaviours. Student evaluation is an objective process and individuals may naturally be 'bad' or 'good' in school activities.

One teacher's comment acknowledges educational inequity among new Canadians but only implicitly. The remark is better read for what it avoids naming rather than for what it does state:

For any discipline, even mathematics, they could try to get books that are made simple. For students who don't have the mathematical background for that level, or they may not have the work background. Something like *Math Made Easy* or *Made Simple*. You could have certain books or pamphlets that emphasize making math simple. That's really what is needed right now for some of these people from other countries. Just to make it a little easier for them; to make the transition from one country to another easier. (R2T3)

Among other points, this teacher has implied several things: that new Canadian students have inferior knowledge and capabilities to European-Canadians, that the responsibility of teaching children with different degrees of exposure to school subjects falls to textbook publishers and not to teachers, that challenges can be eased by providing school work of a simpler level, and that seeking ways to "make it easier" is an appropriate educational goal for students and teachers alike.

These perspectives correspond to researchers' observations of many teachers' conservatism with respect to the causes of educational inequity. For these teachers, the ways that schools structure inequities in the form of differential programs for students are entirely logical. Inequitable practices correspond in these cases to theories about why some people occupy inferior social positions in society (Figueroa 1991; Levine-Rasky 2000a; Ríos 1996; Solorzano and Yosso 2001). Beliefs in individualism, meritocracy, open access to social rewards, and the adequacy of good intentions underlie these educators' legitimation of an inequitable social system. Predictably, they will defend their outlook against disturbance in the form of equity and diversity education.

Other teachers advance a positive outlook on educational inequity without neglecting the fact of social difference [from an interview interaction]:

Q: In your opinion, do students from different racial and ethnic groups have different commitments to education?

A: I'm going to say no. And I'm saying that more and more. The reason I'm going to say no is, I think that you know, people might say that kids from Hong Kong are more committed to education than the general Caucasian, or the general Canadian, you know, I'm referring to people of European background. And, I don't think so, I think there's certainly a large group of European Canadians who are very committed to education and there's a large group from Hong Kong. However, as we see more people coming in from Hong Kong, you're seeing a different attitude; they're just as busy as any dual income, Euro-Canadian and they are leaving it to the school. I think within each culture there are those families who are committed to education and those who are not... . My one Iranian family doesn't seem to be too interested in their child's education but then both parents have full 8-hour day jobs. They're trying to make it in this country, they're trying to rebuild their life and they don't have time. I can give countless examples of Euro-Canadians who are too tired at the end of the day to do anything. (R5T2)

When asked whether some students are given limited educational opportunity because of their race or ethnicity, 33.7% of respondents agree and 46.7% disagree—17.6% are ambivalent. Those who generally subscribe to the opinion that equal opportunities exist for all groups seem to remain unaware of the consequences of the equality of treatment and outcome. Some other respondents refer to patterned variations in educational achievement but in ways that perpetuate stereotypes. Finally, there is a group of teachers who struggle with how to explain educational inequity in a way that resists its unproblematic acceptance.

While variations among European-Canadian educators are observed, educators who are members of racial and ethnic minorities may also mention that the educational outcomes for black children are generally low. Here, the relationship between low academic achievement and racial and ethnic difference strikes a clear outline when teachers refer to students of African-Canadian heritage.

An African-Canadian teacher serves as an example. Her observation of educational inequity is supplemented by her personal knowledge of the African-Canadian experience: "The number of Blacks who view education as a way of moving ahead in society is certainly small in proportion to the white community," she asserts (R1T5).

Such sentiments against African-Canadian students are not limited, of course, to teachers of colour, though remarks of this nature are usually attributed to someone other than oneself:

"Caribbeans are very much against authority. They're never going to make much of themselves because they don't care about education." You know, that kind of thing all the time... . So you have the feeling that these Caribbean students are in your class, but they're troublemakers, you're gonna teach them differently. And if you feel like they're never gonna amount to anything, you don't have any expectations of them. (R2T4)

Reasons teachers give for the educational inequity observed in some groups reveal much about how they construct difference and the meaning they attribute to marginalization. Some reasons rely on sympathetic generalizations about particular groups. Native students, according to one MCE/ARE advisor, have "different concepts of time" and "different values" that meet with educators' disapproval and intolerance, resulting in educational inequity. One respondent registers this belief about "Asian" students: "There isn't any type of person I wouldn't want to have in my class, but the more Asians I get the better. As a culture, they're very motivated" (R4T1).

For some of these respondents, race and ethnicity can converge with family composition and stability. Referring to South Asian (Indo-Pakistani) families, one teacher remarks, "I see totally closer knit families, stability, support systems than a lot of the Jamaican kids have. Consequently, there seems to be a better attitude toward education, school and accomplishments" (R3T1).

Sometimes this pattern merges with what some prefer to regard as "cultural" differences. If, as two explanations assert, Native Canadian students are "very shy" (R4T1), or if Chinese families are led by a mother acting as virtual single parent who commands little authority over her children (R5T1), these cultural predilections obviate teachers' efforts at equity education.

In one interesting explanation for educational differences across groups, a teacher notes but rejects genetic differences claimed in publications such as *The Bell Curve* (Herrnstein and Murray 1995). Still, for this respondent, students' attitudes towards school are somehow culturally disposed: "Some researchers have said that Whites are smarter than Blacks and Asians. I don't believe in that stuff at all. I think it is all cultural; in fact, I do think Asians are taught differently at home than we are culturally" (R1T3). While more liberal in direction, the comment still relies upon gross generalizations of racial and ethnic groups and erects resolute differences between them.

A few respondents reflect the generalization that some racial or ethnic groups instill different degrees of motivation in their children, evaluating this belief as "insensitive" and even "terrible" (R2T3 and R2T7). Sometimes the desire to disqualify generalizations about groups is mitigated by a more benign generalization. "I think certain cultures emphasize certain values. I would go along with that. But I don't think that individuals are for me that drastically different. I know a lot of them do certain things and a generation later they change" (R4T4). This speaker entertains a notion of social difference that admits flexibility, although the association between patterns of values and particular groups endures.

One teacher struggles with the conflict created when, to her dismay, she finds herself making observations of her Asian students that seem to confirm otherwise unwanted generalizations:

The Oriental children in my class are probably the most committed and the most supported in pushing [they receive] from at home, from the parents and everything. It's a very important part of their family life which is part of the stereotype and I guess I don't like seeing stereotypes confirmed... . The differences within groups are far greater than the differences between groups. There's a higher range. But it's been a little bit upsetting to me, I hate to see anything that confirms a stereotype and it sort of has been like that. (R3T2)

Another teacher voices a similar dilemma: "The kids getting awards for extra-curricular stuff are either east-Asian or white. So I'm saying to myself, there's something wrong here. Is it our fault or their fault or what?" (R3T5). She continues to describe the conflict she has with explaining yet dismissing educational behaviours on the basis of racial or ethnic membership. "The harder you push the kids [there] the more they give you. The harder you push the kids here, they won't come to your class. So that's an interesting question. It bothers me a lot... . There are some students at the school, and I don't know if you can generalize on ethnic background, that don't seem to have the right attitude" (R3T5).

Christine Sleeter (1992b) asserts that the way teachers explain social inequality is the key in determining their perspectives on equity education, especially "what one chooses to attend to, remember, perceive as important and attempt to use" (8). A structural (as opposed to an individualistic) interpretation of inequality is mitigated by these teachers' personal experience of "making it." Lessons from working class personal histories are universalized, but they lack the elements of race, ethnicity, racism, and ethnocentrism that are integral to many other individuals (indeed whole groups') hopes for success.

Factors of race and ethnicity are dismissed as temporary or marginal issues, the effects of which can be overcome with time and effort. Racism and ethnocentrism are not considered vital conditions of social inequality for subordinate groups. Instead, factors like family background, the applicability of education to a family's sense of "making it," intergenerational poverty, self-selection to lower educational streams, the education level of parents, English-language skills, a group's presumed interpretation of the value of schooling, and multiple-intelligence theory (Gardner 1983 and 1999) are all cited by these research respondents when explaining patterns of discrepancies in student achievement. One respondent cited the educational system in the country of origin as creating differences in learning outcomes here in Canada (R5T1).

Some generalizations draw from a range of explanations:

> The failure rate is probably not just due to this school itself, it's probably just as much socio-economic, attitude, work habits, a feeling of frustration, a feeling of "even if I do get a good education there won't be a job for me." (R1T1)

For some teachers, precarious financial circumstances are also related to poor social skills, general disadvantage, or low self-esteem that contributes to poor school performance. The tendency is to sympathetically twin racial and ethnic identity with economic marginality, another form of social inequality that many teachers are relatively comfortable in discussing. A family's concerns for economic "survival" and other issues related to poverty may override those of educational achievement.

One administrator (R1PE) describes discretionary sources of funds or area tax rates that schools may draw upon. Area tax rates provide funds above and beyond the standard transfer payments allotted to schools in that region, but their exact size is determined by the local community. Therefore, schools that serve neighborhoods with residents of high socio-economic status can assure a greater tax revenue than schools that serve working-class districts. Voluntary donations from parents and fund-raising activities further reinforce that advantage, he points out.

One teacher observes, "When I see what goes on in other classes and the advantages that they have and the resources and everything, I'd like to redirect a little bit of that up here" (R3T2).

Some teachers discuss the tensions between sameness and difference, between the denial of racism and observing inequitable treatment of children on the basis of race and ethnicity, or between professional expectations and individual behaviour. These educators regard students as victims of circumstance, specifically those for whom low educational achievement is framed by their membership in a racial or ethnic group. Circumstances may involve the students' economic status, immigration or refugee history, or "cultural" propensities that foster success in North American society. In avoiding generalizations about such students, these teachers face the opposition of a powerful conservative force among their colleagues and, more importantly, among the prevailing ideology that guides education as a whole.

CONSERVATIVE VIEWS ON
RACE, RACISM, AND ANTI-RACISM

Equity and diversity pedagogy is severely criticized by some teachers for focusing on racism, for mobilizing negative forces in classroom practice, and for destroying harmonious social relations among racial groups within schools and the larger society. Some respondents express concern about discussing racism as a "problem" in classroom discourse. In a direct reversal of equity and diversity education principles, politically conservative teachers in this study claim that exposure to race and racism and other forms of oppression may themselves lead to the development of attitudes and behaviours that perpetuate racism.

The belief that equity and diversity education may cause interracial tension mobilizing negative forces in schools emerges in the research of Connolly (1992) and McDonald, Bhavnani, Khan and John (1989) in Britain. The potency of the following statement attributes this source of resistance to equity and diversity:

> I sometimes feel people that are into multicultural education create a racism tension (sic) amongst everybody.... . They get into racial issues, and that gets the stew boiling. I think that sometimes the good intentions are the wrong intentions. As far as I'm concerned, it's creating things that should not be there. (R2T7)

Equity education that is "looking for trouble" should, these teachers say, be abandoned in favour of the more harmonious, benevolent multiculturalism that encourages positive social relations among racial and ethnic groups. It is preferable, one teacher argues, that racism be resolved by "good, structured, moral Christian principles." Awareness of racism is frequently presumed to be unproductive for students and, they advise, should not to be introduced into their consciousness. This belief thrives despite a number of studies revealing that in multiracial societies children are socialized from an early age into a culture that differentiates along racial and ethnic origins (Aboud 1988; Hirschfeld 1996; Rizvi 1993; Troyna and Hatcher 1992).

Some of the resistance to teaching from an equity and diversity framework derives from a sensitivity to the emotions that may be aroused when broaching issues such as inequality, racism and ethnocentrism. If probed, however, this fear may surpass concerns for the sensibilities of marginalized people. It can modulate into serving dominant group interests, specifically in maintaining a self-image that is untainted by participation in systems of oppression.

I don't think it would hurt to teach about the experience of oppression and oppressed people. On the other hand you have to be very careful how you would teach a course like that because you can do the same thing in reverse. By elaborating a situation you, in a sense, create another, like a domino effect. You become free, but you, in a sense, subjugate somebody else with something else. (R5T4)

This teacher echoes the concerns of other respondents. Initially, there is support for equity and diversity education in practice, but after reflection, the speaker cautions against possibility of the tables turning against members who had these good intentions. Such speakers fear that equity and diversity education may create a new group of victims oppressed, presumably, on the basis of some accusation.

The naming of educational inequity that proceeds on the basis of racial or ethnic difference is expected to produce the polarized roles of victim and oppressor. This response corresponds to the role reversal noted earlier in this chapter, in which the dominant cultural group is construed as victim of systematic persecution.

If equity and diversity education is interpreted as one advisor (R5A2) puts it, "the WASP white guilt trip, as banging over the heads with baseball bats for the sins of our forefathers," the belief that equity and diversity education perpetuates systems of exclusion inevitably follows. In role reversal, dominant group members, specifically Whites, become the victims who are erroneously blamed for past wrongdoings in which they had no direct part. They construct a moral position where they will be immune from criticism and accountability. We have seen this response reflected in the claiming of "Canadian" identity, in the fear that the dominant cultural group is excluded from equity and diversity education policy and practice, in the suspicion that racially and ethnically defined groups make unfair claims to economic rewards and public resources, and indeed, in the very way difference is constructed.

The strategy of role reversal is a response to the current rise in the claims, cultures, and hitherto marginalized voices of people of colour in particular. Rather than cede to these claims and listen to these voices, some Whites respond with a retrenchment of their ideological hegemony and social dominance. To sustain their argument, they adopt a viewpoint about the cause of social conflict that exonerates themselves as the socially dominant partner in ongoing power relations.

Groups complaining of inequitable treatment are regarded as causing their own circumstances. "It's them making it an issue," explains one teacher,

"It's the Blacks saying that there is a problem" (R1T3). Whites are able to maintain a position of moral "neutrality," upholding an unexamined belief in what they interpret as liberalism and meritocracy. Liberal beliefs do not demand much from a subscriber until its consequences begin to encroach upon one's personal life. This is experienced as a threat upon one's taken-for-granted privilege.

Others are seen as seeking justification for their inequality through a racialization of the issue "because they don't want to let go of the past; they want it paid for.... It's like the Inquisition" (R2T5). The Black community is held responsible for creating its own circumstances, and is intent, this teacher believes, on "brow-beating itself about its past and about its present position and misperceiving the present position."

Power and privilege are the twin phenomena that must be factored into our analysis if we seek a full understanding of resistance to equity and diversity education. Teachers express trepidation about the prospect of relinquishing their power and privilege in determining the shape of public education in regard to racial and ethnic communities. Ultimately, members of the dominant group are denying fellow citizens their selfhood, self-determination, respect and pluralism (Blauner 1972 and 1989; Feagin and Vera 1995; Stanfield 1991).

Here, one advisor offers a critique on the issues of power and privilege and their relation to the problem of resistance to equity and diversity education:

> Racism is all about power. Power was always put in the hands of a certain people and they become very defensive about that because they don't want to lose that [power]. It is much more comfortable to be in that position to direct other people.... When there is a possibility of losing power they obviously will put up barriers, and it's intentional because they see one group getting more visibility than another. So they want them to slow down and I think that it is intentional. (R1A1)

The impulse to protect (and make decisions from) one's position of power and privilege may manifest itself as an interest in assimilation, according to this advisor, promulgated by the white majority.

Gillborn (1995) also argues that teachers resist equity and diversity education because it threatens the existing power structure. The dominant social group exploits its hegemonic position, its power, in order to ensure its unearned entitlement to such things as educational achievement. In the words of one anti-racism advocate, "racism has to do with the protection of privilege—

people holding on to things, to their traditions, to their status, to the opportunity for economic advancement that they've had based on racial lines, and those are hard things to shake" (Lee 1986, 6).

Investigation of the reasons why educators resist equity and diversity education reveal a great deal about their perspectives on policy, practice, and Professional Development. The pivotal concepts of power and privilege are especially useful in analyzing the distance many educators maintain toward the cultural forms and experiences of marginalized groups. Reliance on an unarticulated power and the privileges that accrue to it inform perspectives on equity and diversity education. Location within the power-privilege structure affects the choices teachers make for their practice, whether they be a nominal gesture or broader revision of the mainstream pedagogy. It provides the contours of school-community relations, whether that be tokenistic, critical, or oppressive. And it shapes the rationale educators offer to excuse themselves from letting the full implications of equity and diversity education bear upon their own identity and moral framework.

ENDNOTES

1. In secondary school, "General" level courses do not qualify students for university, unlike courses offered at the "Advanced" level.

chapter three

Educators' Perspectives
and Practices

EDUCATORS' RESPONSES TO EQUITY AND
DIVERSITY POLICIES AND PRACTICES

There is a gap between hopes for equity in education and the realization of equity in actual outcomes. In exploring research findings on teachers' perspectives on difference, forms of exclusion, and educational inequity, we begin to traverse that gap. What teachers believe and understand about these issues reveals a great deal about the obstacles equity and diversity advocates face. Perspectives and practices in equity and diversity education reflect conservative approaches.

This chapter describes teachers' general perspectives on equity and diversity policy and education and then focuses on their self-reported approach to classroom activities. Broader practices that circumscribe school, board, parent community involvement, and professional development are addressed as we negotiate our way over that chasm separating hope from reality. It is after a thorough look at what fills the chasm that we may begin to reinvigorate efforts to draw the two sides together.

The policies, task force reports, and action plans of the five school boards studied bear a striking resemblance to each other (see *School Boards' Policies* in Appendix C). Each contain minor variations upon the same themes, which include, but are not restricted to: the production of bias-free curriculum materials; the condemnation of racial and ethnic bias within the school environment; the development of culturally appropriate assessment that is sensitive to students' racial and ethnic backgrounds; staff development to encourage the necessary awareness and skills to work competently in a *diverse* environment; employment equity policies inclusive of race, culture, ethnicity, etc. and finally, working towards an environment where parents, the school and the community are all involved in the schooling process.

All school districts in our study have policies on equity and diversity education. However, teachers are often unaware of the policy, or refer to its low profile in their work environment. Associated with the discomfort in discussing issues of race and educational inequality, equity policies sometimes elicit silence rather than discussion:

I don't think it's something that is discussed among teachers. (R5T4)

If there is a policy, it's probably talked about in other departments. I don't go to those meetings because I'm in Special Ed. (R4T5)

Nobody has highlighted multicultural policy or mentioned it. It's hardly mentioned here in the school setting. (R5T1)

Professional conduct is assumed to ensure appropriate responses to equity and diversity as this speaker claims:

I think they'd probably guess that there was one. They don't know, they wouldn't know what it is specifically, but we are trained in all these, we look at our culture as teachers... we're very accepting of each other as well, so it sort of falls off the framework that comes with the kind of professionals that we have here. (R5T6)

Ignorance or dismissal of policy by educators may indicate a larger problem. Below, one MCE/ARE advisor links vagueness with the marginalization of equity education:

No organization has yet, to my knowledge, really conceptualized what anti-racism education is. It's usually done on the periphery, on the margin of the organization. And overall, a great deal of lip service is paid, but it never finds its way into the heart of the organization. So accountability is a real issue. (R2A1)

Another sees organizations' administrators as simply engaging in "politically correct" behaviours:

For many principals and superintendents it is the politically correct thing to do. And hence, carry it out as a fellowship when they do it. (R3A1)

When teachers do refer to policy, it may be interpreted narrowly, for establishing appropriate holiday activities, for example, or as a reaction to racial conflicts:

> If we don't have Christmas, what about the traditional Canadian Christmas? I mean that's not good, we're not having that. We also have a backlash of people saying, "I think you've got to have respect for all the other cultures." So that's an issue that isn't resolved. I wish it were. I wish we had a policy on it. (R5T6)

> There are no knife fights in the hallways. You get one knife fight going and we'd have a policy. (R5T6)

> The [provincial] government makes it very clear that we are trying to work with kids who learn at different rates and learn in different ways. I think that government initiative and philosophy, which is totally accepted at the elementary level, is the biggest support of multiculturalism. I don't think the Board has felt it necessary to go any further than that. (R5T6)

Echols and Fisher (1992) confirm that teachers are reluctant to deal with issues of race and racism in policy and practice. In their study, school action plans declared that policy should focus on multiculturalism rather than race relations, or called for an emphasis on "the positive" rather than any attempt to "diffuse racial tensions." Staff resent the use of the term "race," fearing that calling attention to race could incite conflict. The greatest reason for rejecting racism in favor of multiculturalism is "a stated or evidenced faith in a vision of the contemporary community and nation as being a basically fair, liberal, pluralism 'melting pot of cultures' " (1992, 71). Echols and Fisher conclude that the impact of equity education policy is negligible on the lives of students, and that schools' construction of action plans are merely in compliance with district policy directives.

When equity and diversity education is translated into popular educational discourse, it generally assumes the form of multicultural and anti-racism education. Generally speaking, multicultural education (MCE) is regarded as a positive and preventative approach to equity education, while anti-racist education is regarded as a negative or reactive approach to undesirable situations.

Indeed, more respondents (37.8%) were ambivalent about the statement, "The term 'anti-racism' should be replaced because it is negative," than those who agreed (33.5%), or those who disagreed (27%) with it. Several excerpts illustrate these views:

I think with MCE you're trying to include a lot of things from other cultures. Being sensitive to their holidays so that when they're absent on those days you make allowances for that. Whereas anti-racism is more negative. If you hear comments then you might want to deal with those. (R2T4)

MCE is when you're trying to help kids preserve and celebrate their identities, as diverse as they may be. And certainly working with these identities towards the goal of working together within Canada to make a cohesive group. ARE again, is recognizing our differences, but being able to live with the differences ... and working with kids so that they can live with the differences and respect kids in a way that they're not hurtful towards other children. (R3T7)

One is a more positive approach and one is sort of focusing on the negative. Like, multiculturalism you're trying to emphasize strength and [with] anti-racism you're dealing with negativists, trying to erase actual negative viewpoints. (R4T6)

One teacher in our study admits discomfort with the "negativity" implied by anti-racist education but suggests the need for it nonetheless:

MCE is the education of all cultures and what is positive. ARE, I do have problems with the word. I would assume [that we] should dwell on the fact that we attempt to teach students and educate them in the field of anti-racism; how in fact anyone in any world can turn around and say I am not racist... . We are in a society that propagates it. I think what we have to do in education is sit back and learn to deal with my racism and allow this process to help me through it. (R1T6)

How do teachers regard the relationship between MCE and ARE? For some, the two mesh but in almost unintentional ways:

In social studies when I actually do a unit on multiculturalism I'm focusing on celebrating the differences and how "Together we're better" like the poster I have up in my room says. And I will comment at the same time on racist comments or racist actions. There are things that come up in the news that we'll discuss in the classroom. (R4T2)

I would say that MCE if done right should include anti-racism. (R5T6)

Sometimes the two are deliberately integrated:

[MCE and ARE are] very related. I cannot say they're two different things because in a multicultural society you have to implement strategies—anti-racist strategies—in the classroom. (R4T7)

For those who do make a distinction between MCE and ARE, the goals and underlying assumptions of each are also distinguishable (see Table 3.1):

Multiculturalism is a very positive sense of embracing and understanding and accepting and celebrating our differences with recognition that we

---

Table 3.1
Teachers' Responses to the Goals of Multicultural and Anti-racist Education

Valid percent

Item	Agree/ Strongly Agree	Disagree/ Strongly Disagree	Ambivalent	n
The goal of multicultural education (MCE) is to encourage respect for a diversity of cultural traditions.	94.2	1.2	3.5	991
The goal of MCE is to include diverse cultural norms, values and traditions as part of the mainstream curriculum.	72.4	9.8	16.0	986
The goal of anti-racist education (ARE) is to change individual behaviours and attitudes that reinforce racism.	89.3	3.6	5.7	988
The goal of ARE is to change institutional policies and practices that perpetuate racism.	87.3	4.3	9.6	984

---

are more similar than we are different, and that's my interpretation. They come together for all these things, we're all different, yet there are parts of us that are all the same, a very sort of apple pie kind of statement. The very Canadian sense, we are different and you're allowed to be different and you're encouraged to be different. Because of our multicultural fabric, elements of racism converge because of impact really. (R5T7)

Other researchers have also found that teachers perceive anti-racist education as confrontational and inducing guilt for members of dominant cultural groups (Aboud and Doyle 1996; Gillborn 1995; Greenman, Bannan, Kimmel and Radford-Curry 1992). Yet some teachers in our study argue for an ARE approach over MCE:

> Multiculturalism, I always think of fairs where you learn about different cultures and at this level at elementary it ends up being a fun thing. And it can be dangerous because it ends up a Ha Ha, what a fun thing to do, what a funny thing to wear, what a funny thing to eat, and it's almost like a Halloween type of festival. Anti-racism is a whole different agenda. I think giving the term "anti-racism" is saying that racism exists and we know it. It's there and we have to work against it. That's more of an agenda of trying to get everybody to get along and sort of show where people are coming from, where they are presently, and where we have to go. Where cultural relations [are concerned] I think anti-racism has to come first and the multiculturalism can be put in alongside. (R1T3)

We discovered both tremendous support for and criticism of MCE and ARE among teachers. The following anecdotes show both extremes. One secondary school teacher (R2T5) vehemently objects to the entire premise of anti-racism for fear of instilling in students a dangerous attitude about social inequality between the various social groups encountered in the school. Anti-racism, according to this teacher, defeats the purpose of MCE by focusing on racism and the effects of social differences between groups. The goal of MCE is the development of harmonious social relations between groups who come to a common "peoplehood" only upon an absolute and ironic *erasure* of difference. For this teacher, anti-racism is the domain of opinions and attitudes while MCE is the domain of experience. It is an approach supremely more qualified to provide students with the resources to attain the goal of equity education. MCE conveys to students the universality of "human nature" and encourages them to assimilate difference into their own moral frameworks, while ARE threatens to disintegrate any semblance of this harmonious appearance.

The views of an elementary school teacher stand in contrast to the secondary school teacher represented above. She describes the evolution of her thought about the need for ARE in the schools. Her initial response to the anti-racist statement promulgated by her Board was one of shock, then suspicion about its accuracy. She then notes that the statement served to raise her consciousness about the reality of racism and motivated her to take some proactive steps toward equity in her own practice. Now, she says:

> The content of the curricular program should change because the social fabric of the society is full of different cultures and different approaches to life and different religions and different ways of thinking. And I believe that this should now be an obligation, a part of the curriculum, in order to prepare the kids to really live the challenge of the diversity. (R3T3)

This sentiment echoes that of another teacher who states that "equity curriculum is the basis of all curriculum." For these teachers, the responsibility of the school to respond to diversity reaches beyond its role to prepare students for further learning or for the workplace. In the words of one respondent, it is a question of, "How are we going to become new citizens of a new society?" Yet another teacher's insight indicates that the challenge entails an entirely new vision of the educator's role. How this vision is to be formed and how it is to be realized are questions that demand considerable attention.

Among school administrators, one finds a greater familiarity with MCE and ARE than that possessed by many teachers. In distinguishing them, one (R4PE) states that MCE focuses on the uniqueness of each culture and their differences but criticizes this approach for its emphasis on a folkloric and stereotypical notion of culture. This administrator recognizes that such programs, in emphasizing the static, romanticized differences between social groups, resist the acknowledgment of racism as the source of social inequality for groups. ARE, on the other hand "is very different in that it is far more proactive in dealing with attitudes and behaviours of kids towards other groups."

While supportive of ARE and its objectives, another administrator only understands it as addressing individual attitudes and behaviours in addition to particular curricular materials. He makes no mention of the need to examine structural inequalities or the school's hidden curriculum as it is engendered in differential teacher expectations.

Teachers who interpret equity and diversity education as a discrete pedagogical activity or as applicable only to certain disciplines, tended to resist its application to their regular practice. Among those interviewed were two secondary teachers of mathematics who may serve as examples. Both expressed serious doubts and uncertainty about whether MCE and ARE could be implemented in their classrooms. A particularly provocative quote from one is useful here:

> What am I going to be discussing [anti-racist education] for? Where's it actually going to come up? I can see it in social studies, I can see in English, but the only reason I would be bringing it up is because I think my classroom is racist, right? That would be the only reason because it doesn't correspond with parabolas in any sense. Maybe it does. Maybe parabolas are racist against circles, I don't know. (R5T3)

Comments such as these indicate a parochial interpretation of the intent of MCE and ARE. Teachers tend to read them for their curricular application as an additive or corrective to their already established pedagogical methods. If they were to implement MCE or ARE, these respondents believe that they would have to learn about the contributions of prominent individuals who are members of minority groups, in effect revamping the curriculum so the new information may be integrated.

What is really required, however, is not a piecemeal revision of classroom teaching. It is the process *and* the content of teaching that needs to be examined, an exercise that is foreign to many educators. The math teacher ends up with the fact that there is, "nothing within the course that is actually based on any race or culture." When teaching is constructed as the conveyance of objective information devoid of values or social implications, no other conclusion *is* possible. Anti-racism cannot easily fit into her approach to the learning experience.

These responses reflect teachers' inaccurate or incomplete understanding of the intent of MCE and ARE as expressed by its advocates. Comments such as the following are quite common:

> It is like additional responsibilities, which tend to be a burden. (R2T4)

It would just be another thing for me to have to, you know, try and figure out where I'm going to fit this in, or I guess you do a little bit every day, but the days are already packed, I find. (R5T3)

These educators interpret MCE and ARE as just another curricular innovation they are expected to add to their already full programs rather than an orientation to the teaching and learning process that informs their regular activities. In addition, they are seen within the pedagogical framework known as the transmission model of instruction in which the teacher is a master of knowledge who passes it to those without knowledge. If MCE and ARE imply the acquisition of new knowledge or factual material, then teachers conclude they are being asked to insert yet more material in their already full repertoires.

In conforming to the traditional curriculum guidelines, these teachers believe either that the core curriculum does not lend itself to equity and diversity education, or that the school program is too full to accommodate issues such as equity and diversity, which are perceived to be peripheral. The following statement represents these views:

Math, for example is sort of a straightforward subject, you don't really do it [make connections with equity and diversity education]. In geography, in history we have a curriculum to adhere to. And the curriculum in history is the American Revolution, the growth of Canada, Confederation. All the immigrants at those points were British, French, Scandinavian, German, so you know... the curriculum is overcrowded as it is. (R2T1)

Another common concern for teachers is "curricular overload." This is an important dimension of the actual conditions of work for teachers. In this common form of resistance, educators complain of overwhelming demands on their time, implying that equity and diversity education is yet another thing to add to their already full program.

Teachers name a wide range of competing programs and initiatives to which they are expected to adapt while maintaining a day-to-day routine for their students. They report feeling challenged, even overwhelmed by the new pedagogical mandates that compete for credibility and implementation:

So here you have a staff overworked, under tremendous pressure. People generally think they're lazy and don't work hard enough anyway and now you want them to be sensitive and aware? That's change in itself. I don't think so. (R4T6)

Education is being asked to do a lot of things nowadays. And the average teacher throws their arms up. You know, what's next? The teacher nowadays, especially in elementary, has many different roles. Not only teacher, but also social worker, doctor, father, mother, because of the high divorce rate. Like in my class this year, half of the kids come from divorced parents and that's another problem you have to deal with. All the changes that are going on in education nowadays. You've got drugs, and of course, the racial thing. (R2T2)

Some teachers respond to this competition of priorities by returning to some semblance of autonomy over their own classrooms. They select out from the current multiplicity of directives those programs that correspond to their personal feelings about the role and the purpose of education. Some feel that they have no other choice, given how they view their roles and responsibilities.

This perspective is not limited to teachers. An advisor describes the quandary that teachers face in this "showdown" of curricular overload:

This society appears to be developing a lot of problems and there doesn't seem to be anybody out there to combat those problems. So teachers are coming under a lot of pressure to not only make sure that kids are able to read, but they also have to make sure that they have to be the nurse, the psychologist, the parent, the global citizen, the ecology freak. You know, they have to be all these things and it's putting a very big burden on the education system. (R5A2)

The question of the applicability of MCE and ARE in schools serving both homogeneous and heterogeneous neighborhoods is a topic many educators respond to at length. Some support the programs regardless of the nature of the student population, and others support it conditionally. They make a point of stating their unequivocal support even in schools characterized by a largely white population.

Others support ARE only when it is "called for" in reacting to and resolving racial conflicts, a situation more likely to arise in schools with some cultural diversity to begin with. To this effect, one teacher states that ARE would be necessary if "we had problems at this schools [sic] where students were picking on students and ridiculing whatever culture they're from. But we don't seem to have that here. People seem to get along pretty well.... If it isn't broken, don't fix it" (R2T2). A MCE/ARE advisor anticipates this response:

> Well, I think a lot of them say they don't see the need [for MCE and ARE] because they don't have racially visible people within their community or handicapped children, or children lacking language development. So therefore why are we putting efforts into this area when we don't have a problem? (R1A1)

Other teachers would not concur with the opinion cited above. They make the point that MCE and ARE have a necessary place in all schools in all districts. This position is consistent with the survey, in which over 85% of respondents either disagreed or disagreed strongly that MCE and ARE, respectively, are necessary only in schools in which there is great racial or ethnic diversity.

Teachers are sensitive at least to the rhetoric of equity in education as the appropriate concern of all schools regardless of demographics. This sentiment is demonstrated in this comment:

> I think there are far [more] problems with racism and the need for anti-racism in their [middle-class, monocultural] school and I could never get them to agree with that. And I think my children are missing out. I think their education is flawed and weak and uncolourful, and they're the ones who are missing out. This is a much richer and a much more realistic education here that's going to prepare these kids for life. And so I really resent it when people think that you should only be interested in ARE and MCE in the north end or the south end [of the Board with rich diversity] and forget about [the] central [homogeneous area]. (R3T2)

Teachers' perspectives on equity and diversity education are often idiosyncratic. Views range widely with respect to what is meant by MCE and ARE, their respective purposes and their degree of overlap. This range is true of administrators as well. Since evaluations of MCE and ARE are contingent upon perspectives, their application in the classroom encounters considerable difficulty. It is not at all clear to educators how or if equity and diversity education relates to what they normally do. Many are thus reluctant to advance the cause of equity and diversity education. The next section describes how these perspectives are manifested in classrooms.

CLASSROOM PRACTICES

Classroom activities oriented around multicultural and anti-racist themes vary widely according to teachers' perspectives and individual preferences. Here, there is a prime opportunity to gain insight into how thoroughly a teacher has penetrated the pedagogic possibilities inherent in MCE and ARE.

Practices are based upon commitment, and commitment reveals everything about one's current level of understanding of MCE and ARE. An observer of Canadian teachers' classroom practices would discover a generally unsystematic, serendipitous implementation of equity education. Many interesting individual examples are listed below, selected from the data:

- Conducting a Chinese New Year's parade initiated entirely by a classroom group;
- Discussing with the children the inaccuracy and symbolic meanings of black and white paint pigments and other art materials when representing oneself;
- International literature in a secondary school English class is used to facilitate the "perception of specific cultures in South Africa," albeit from a colonial perspective (using Laurens Van der Post's *A Walk with the White Bushman*, 1986);
- Seeking out images of racial/ethnic minority groups in texts that purposely defeat stereotypes;
- The original reader in a grade 2-3 class is changed to one that reflects racial and ethnic diversity;
- Various activities adapted to include social difference, such as the translation of a song into the languages represented by the children and a racially mixed group project concerning the writing and illustration of a story;
- An overall approach to a personal version of ARE in which "We recognize difference in a positive way. I use it as my base to build self-esteem. Each child's identity is validated ... if that is race, ethnicity, class or gender. From that point we are empowered activists ready to claim our rightful place in society";
- Discussing the meaning of racism including appropriate responses for children upon hearing racist jokes and slurs.

In search of patterns across the data, the first preference to arise is teachers' reliance on students' initiation of issues associated with equity. These teachers implement a version of equity and diversity education only when students spontaneously raise related issues:

It's an issue that we discuss when we read or we study like ancient history and African studies and all that. In grade 11 History we touch on slavery and anytime a student brings up something I deem appropriate we discuss it, and it happens very often. I don't have to adapt [MCE/ARE] because the course I'm teaching allows students to comment, question, and debate issues and they bring it up. (R1T2)

The reliance upon student initiative and motivation may be interpreted by some educators as consistent with student-centered teaching in which students are invited to participate more fully in directing their own learning experiences. They may be asked to act as learning resource not only for each other but also for the teacher, who may respond by relinquishing authority over teaching. This is particularly useful, even necessary, when a teacher does not share the same set of cultural ideas and history as the students. From this perspective, students' active involvement embodies equity and diversity education. Yet gaps between this approach and a full integration of equity and diversity education into teachers' pedagogy are noticeable:

We tend to deal primarily with social issues that of course directly come from them [students] and that doesn't necessarily come from me. You have to understand that the process classroom does not allow it to be contrived. At the same time it will come from them, but in actuality the underlying meaning comes from me. (R1T6)

They walk into [music class] with their Walkmans, and I ask, "What are you listening to?" And I ask them to bring it over and I listen to it. And I have to go out and buy recordings of this stuff because you always have to go from what they know to what they don't know. So I have to learn. So it's a whole new learning experience for me. I know that best products of musical expression are from Western European society from what I know right now. To me, the ethnic stuff that I've heard, and I haven't heard very much, seems to be a lot less sophisticated. And if they start bringing that stuff in, that to me will possibly lower the content or quality of my program. (R3T5)

Another set of responses to equity and diversity education in classroom practice concerns the accommodation of different cultures in traditional school practices. This approach represents the inclusion of racial or ethnic groups' experiences into a class or school project. It does not entail the adoption of a qualitatively new project but rather an expansion of one already in use. Moreover, what is nominally included is usually some non-western cultural symbol such as a holiday ritual or performance in a broad sense. For example:

> I have a project. It's on cultural awareness. I have 7 or 8 children in my group and they're all from different ethnic backgrounds. I train them to dance all kinds of dance. I do research in the community, I interview people to learn the basic dance steps and I learn it with the parents with me as an officer I trained them to do different dances, but a Filipino will dance a Native dance. Like anyone whose done any dance that's not their own dance, in order for them to appreciate the beauty of the culture of other racial groups. And I found it very effective. (R4T7)

Despite the predominance of limited uses of equity and diversity education, some educators are willing to embark upon a more unconventional experience for students. The following example describes the planning of specific types of educational activities and experiences outside of the classroom. A broader appreciation of difference seems to be the objective:

> I treat all students the same. I try to appeal to the compassion of the students. I try to get students to understand how they would feel if they were the minority, put themselves in the other person's shoes. I try to encourage the "global village" attitude, the need to be multinational. I have an international perspective. I try to connect their lives with the real world. I try to get everybody to mix. I take them on field trips, skiing trips, and overseas field trips. I try to work from both perspectives—mainstream kids and new arrivals. In my homeroom, I try to promote internationalism. I teach them about Chinese culture. There's an affectionate relationship among my students, regardless of their racial or ethnic origin. (R5T1)

Finally, we arrive at teaching practices that emphasize the more challenging aspects of equity and diversity education. This example describes classroom dialogue about racism as it dovetails with family histories, literature, and white supremacy groups respectively:

> We just finished a project just recently; the Elimination of Racism Day. We brainstormed and we watched some movies, *Ernest Greene Story* and

we had already seen Sylvia Hamilton's film, *Speak from the Heart of Black Nova Scotia*, and we also watched *The Long Walk Home*. And we looked at stereotyping and racism, "red neck," and we had all kinds of definitions. We talked about boycott and looked at all those issues. I gave them a project; they could write a response to the movies, or they could do an advertisement for a movie, but they had to show in it that they were against segregation, or discrimination, or stereotypes so it had to reflect one of those themes we have done. (R1T5)

For those teachers willing to accommodate equity and diversity education to their classroom practices, the need for teaching and learning resources and materials is no obstacle. In one case, finding resources is regarded as uncomplicated and a matter of course even when extra effort is required. In another case, the provision of learning resources is simply there for the asking. Whether teachers avail themselves of the opportunity is the question:

Most of what I do, I do myself. I take the initiative to get as many books as I can, buying for the classroom. I don't deal with it as a separate thing so it's part of it; it's kind of just using my own resources in terms of discussion. I try to make an effort to get out of the libraries also for my own thing. (R3T2)

One principal reports reliance upon resources from the area's black cultural centre during a grade 4 unit on pioneers because the black community in the region dates back to these times; the local white community does not.

Teachers who are more hesitant to implement equity and diversity education in their classrooms find the availability of resources problematic. They are unwilling to make the effort to identify the resources available or specify how one might find them. They seem unaware of the possibility of utilizing administrative, board, or community facilities to aid them in this task. In addition, some will disregard materials or projects that are not specifically designated in the standard curriculum guideline:

I've come across very little in terms of really good textbook stuff or good activities. So basically you're creating that yourself... but I think if it's too hard for people to do, they're bound not to do it or less likely to do it. (R4T2)

In this section, we have seen how teachers resist and accommodate equity and diversity education in their classroom practices. The reader may be tempted to say that there are as many forms of implementation as there are teachers. Teaching practice is, in many ways, individualistic. But regarding teaching as nothing more than individualistic limits an analysis of the visible patterns.

It is apparent that teachers are not tackling the more important aspects of equity and diversity education. While topics of stereotypes and the oppression attending immigration are discussed in some classrooms, the difficult circumstances of students' lives today are typically neglected. Culture generally connotes a static symbol of difference often in the form of an extant ritual or art form. The revision of traditional teaching, evaluation, or management skills receives little or no mention. How does equity and diversity education fare at the level of school or school board activities? The next section discusses these findings.

SCHOOL AND BOARD PRACTICES

Specific projects developed at the school and board level may assume the quality of a compensatory approach to MCE. Schools may, for example, undertake projects to help schools in developing nations. In another enrichment approach, students may be exposed to children from schools in more diverse areas. Interpersonal and communication skills are emphasized in such projects as a camp for mediation resolution or multicultural leadership training. Other schoolwide projects involved celebrations in which social difference was the organizing theme.

While Multicultural Weeks are common practice in some boards, they are not universal. One principal dismisses the value of Multicultural Week because its purpose becomes diluted as just another weekly theme. Several educators criticize a ubiquitous Multicultural Week as a sloganized celebration of diversity without lasting effect. One adviser states that even adopting multiculturalism as a year-long theme is "a flash in the pan; it's like 'We've done it, been there. Let's move on.'" Another administrator organizes a school assembly on the topic of their anti-racist policy, but does not promote a school event devoted to the theme. "I think the danger is," he explains, " if you have a big initiative, then when it's over people think anti-racism is over, and I would rather build it into the infrastructure of the school." (R3PE)

This individual's critique of Multiculturalism Week, above, is not consistent with his overall school plan despite his evaluation of his school as being a "very politically correct situation" (R1PE). Pressed to suggest ways in which his school could change sources of educational inequality and ethnocentrism specifically, the limitations of his approach to MCE are made evident. This

Teaching for Equity and Diversity

principal admitted his ignorance; he could not suggest any appropriate classroom activities.

In another case, a principal notes the relatively low priority of equity and diversity education: "If the superintendent phoned and said, 'Listen, you're getting an extra $50,000,' to suggest that I would be prepared to put that straight into MCE, no I probably wouldn't." (R3P5)

The problem of uncommitted leadership is a serious one (Allcott 1992; Solomon 2002). Alcott found that the progress of introducing equity and diversity education into a school is highly influenced by the administrator. A teacher remarks upon the importance of the school administrator assuming an unequivocally supportive role in the adoption of equity and diversity programs:

> It helps if you have an administration that says, "Hey, let's look at a new way of doing this, or handling this." Our administrator is very open that way and he allows change; sometimes he tries to institute it, but most times he likes to think that it comes from within. He is constantly seeking new ways for an approach which is positive for us because when we find a new approach we are not in a threatening situation. (R1T6)

The centrality of their role aside, caution must be exercised before school administrators are evaluated, to whether they are more accommodating than teachers with regard to equity and diversity education. One teacher reports this abrupt end to a multicultural project she would have initiated:

> Another thing we'd like to get going in the school, is having welcome signs in all the different languages at the entrance of our school and again, it's just been time and I haven't been able to get it done. But, one of the fellows at the School Board Office called a couple of principals about having this done for all of the schools. Instead of relying on someone like me to try and get it done in paper at my school, they would make them available for all schools. He called three principals who did not want that. I'd doubt they'd tell you that, but that was his experience. (R5T2)

This flaw reflects the fact that administrators, even apparently enlightened ones, filter information about MCE and ARE through their personal moral and interpretive lenses. One of the administrator's roles is to act as liaison between the school and the public, necessitating correspondence between public values and those represented by the institution. Because they must cater to these and other often-contradictory mandates (Solomon 2002), school administrators are not more likely than anyone else to align themselves with staunch equity and diversity education proponents.

Some other tensions were expressed about modifying traditional school practices to accommodate students of diverse racial and ethnic groups. These included Christmas programs that better respond to the diversity of their students. In our survey item, "Christmas celebrations are threatened by other cultural traditions," 28.5% agreed, 57.6% disagreed, and 12.3% were ambivalent. While 63.4% of survey respondents agreed, "it is important to ensure that school symbols, songs, decorations, logos and celebrations reflect the racial/ethnic diversity of the school population," 18% disagreed, with 17.6% remaining ambivalent.

Yet when we listen to the concerns of individual teachers, the tension between the way teachers present themselves in the survey and their actual feelings are heard:

> The thing with Christmas—that has been a big issue. People come from other countries and here we're adapting to them instead of them adapting to us. So that has been a thing that has bugged teachers over the years. We can have a Christmas program, but don't do Christmas songs and don't mention Christmas and the whole bit. Instead of just having black (sic), instead of recognizing one group, we should recognize everybody. (R2T2)
>
> The principal announced that it was Black History Month. And when we do "Show & Tell" a couple of the kids—I believe one was a black girl—said, "What's this Black History Month?" And so I explained that I believe that what the principal was saying is that we're taking a month to recognize black people and what their culture has brought to Canada. And another child said, "Why black?" And I said, "That's a question I ask too. Why don't we just make it Multicultural Month and recognize that everybody is special instead of just Blacks?" (R2T2)

This last case (speaker R2T2) is interesting to follow because it elucidates the schools' inconsistent undertaking of "Black History Month" despite the principal's ostensible commitment to it:

> So I talked with the principal later and said, "Why is it Black History Month?" And he said that's the directive that comes down from the

Superintendent. And his statement was that we're to do that and if we don't like it then we should move on. I thought that was a pretty strong statement to make. But anyway, not really any more came of it in the month as time passed. I thought, "What kind of push are we going to get on this?" But it was just announced a couple of times that it's Black History Month. That upset me and some other teachers. Why can't it be Multicultural Month, which would make more sense. (R2T2)

Another teacher reports an exchange between herself and a teacher who expressed resistance to the school's undertaking of Black History Month:

He said Canadian students were saying, "Why can't they have a day when they celebrate Canadian history, and why should Blacks be given the privilege when they've never had a white assembly in the school?" They are placed as minority, because the Blacks were given maybe the upper hand over them. So if the teacher isn't wise enough to know what sort of response to give to students like this, they just encourage that type of thinking... I did say to the teacher that probably what you should have said was that they have a white assembly every day. Because the Canadian cultural and history is sort of common knowledge, everybody knows about it. But for the Blacks, because they have sort of a hidden history and it's just being brought to light, the assembly is mainly for educational purposes. (R3T6)

Responses to MCE and ARE schoolwide programs that reflect limited support from teachers are not the only pattern to note. When called for, entire approaches to the curriculum are dramatically altered at some schools to suit the objectives of MCE and ARE. In one case, a school administrator (R4PE) points out how he had made substantive changes to the ways holidays were now celebrated in his school so as to better reflect the interests of the diverse student body. Each class in the school now chooses a different cultural group at the beginning of the school year and interprets each holiday according to the traditions of that group. In this school, Thanksgiving Day has become the Festival of Harvest, a theme common to many groups. Halloween became the Festival of Superstition. Christmas was revised as the Festival of Light and so on. One teacher there now highlights the school's anti-racist theme in Remembrance Day, for example, when it is presented as "what happens when racism is taken to the limit."

It is simple to support equity and diversity education in principle. Everyone has good intentions. But, as Hamilton (1996) found in her study of a school in the American Midwest, good intentions are insufficient to produce the actual infusion of principles into perspectives and practices in the schools. There *is* much to applaud in individual teachers' and even larger school efforts to be inclusive and equitable to all children. Yet a closer look at particular attitudes about MCE and ARE uncovers many areas of concern. One is that of parent and community relations. The discussion that follows reveals the work to be done in this area.

PARENT AND COMMUNITY INVOLVEMENT IN SCHOOLING

In what ways are parents encouraged to join the activities of the school? Types of contributions are related to the diversity of the individual school and to its orientation toward equity and diversity education, particularly the support given to this principle by the teaching staff. In a school where equity and diversity education are actively pursued, parents' input is critical and influential.

In one case, parents contribute to the writing of a school code that concerns human rights and anti-racism. In another school with a relatively low level of diversity, the parent group is uninvolved with issues of equity and diversity. Yet another parent group helps promote a school's themes of "peace education, self-esteem and discipline and conflict resolution," but the principal has mobilized these prerogatives, not the parents themselves. The principal points out that these parents do not have sufficient influence over the curriculum nor do they occupy positions of leadership. The parents take their cue from the administrator, who often determines the kind of parental involvement in the school.

Support for parent involvement is not always expressed, regardless of what teachers "should" think. The anticipation of backlash from dominant cultural groups may justify some teachers' resistance to inviting participation from parents who are members of various racial and ethnic groups:

> There's a sense that education is suffering because of all the groups we have let into Canada. And "My kid's not getting x number of instructional hours because you have to instruct and talk about Somalia or Poland and that means that my child is not learning his ABCs." (R3T7)

Fear of backlash from dominant cultural groups is not without justification. In one school in which December holiday celebrations were revised to include a Hindu tradition, parents of European background organized themselves to express their criticism. They were vehement about exposing different celebrations to their own children but were unable to see the effect of imposing European traditions on others.

Obstacles to teachers utilizing community members and parents as learning resources include lack of knowledge, or inaccessibility, cost, and general unwillingness:

> There's no ready translating service at school. They make no use of resources in the community for translators though the Board does. The attitude is that where would we stop? We would have to translate every language in the district. We need home-school workers to do this or to help parents find a person to translate or interpret them. What they do is mark a notice with a sticker that the children take home that needs to be translated and then it's up to the parents to get it translated by someone, but this is ineffective I think. They did talk about employing home-school workers, but I seem to recall they wanted highly specialized, academically trained people who were too expensive to hire. (R5T1)

Despite these reservations, the surrounding community may play a part in classroom activities even when an individual teacher might be quite unsure what to make of the experience:

> We went to a Sikh temple once and I heard some music and I was talking to the people there. But it will be a different thing, because it comes from a different culture you know, just to sit down and listen to music for its own sake is different from their experience. But I'm totally ignorant about this. (R3T5)

Sampling the culturally different is a popular approach for teachers interested in using the community as a resource to teach about equity and diversity. This finding is corroborated by Echols and Fisher (1992, 68). These experiences, however, are generally devoid of social and historical contexts that could evoke discussion of critical issues. Community members may be invited into the school to speak, not of a racial or ethnic group's experience with racism or discrimination in society, but of the presumed fixed cultural traits that are expected to help teachers in "understanding" their students. While this information may be important, it may come to represent the sum total of a teacher's knowledge of social difference, even serving to confirm negative expectations of some groups. The chance for a racially or ethnically defined group to introduce alternative viewpoints or to elaborate on the implications of growing up in Canadian society is slim.

Parents from ethnically or racially defined communities may be encouraged to contribute to classroom and school activities but usually in terms set by teachers and their administrators. The extent of their involvement is often restricted to the elaboration or confirmation of absolute cultural differences in the form of religious observance, traditions in music, dance, and so on.

Sometimes they may be called upon to explain students' perplexing social behaviour to teachers. Despite these reports of participation in the schools, parents are held responsible for their children's educational inequality. It is ironic that parents are denied power and control over school affairs but blamed for not having enough involvement in their children's schooling.

One teacher explains, for example, that some parents are afraid to confront a teacher and they avoid discussing school problems with their children. As a result, their children dismiss the importance of trying to do well in school. From this perspective, social difference is defined as the problem. This may involve racial or ethnic group membership, as well as social markers of educational inequality such as low-income, single parent families, disempowerment, complicity, and alienation from the schools. These interview excerpts convey the ways in which parents "choose" their subordination even while their struggles are acknowledged:

> The question is how you get them to play a more active role and this is what we're struggling with. A lot of these parents are single parents. They're both working in some cases. They don't have time or see the importance of school. They just sort of turn their children over to the school and it's our responsibility to deal with them while they're here. (R3T1)

> You'll send a report card home. You don't hear a thing. If the parents aren't concerned, you phone home and mom and dad will say, "Well, there's just nothing I can do." Well I don't find that enough support. (R5T3)

Low parental involvement and teachers' resistance to meaningful parent involvement is a paradox that calls attention to itself. On the one hand, parent participation is desirable, even essential. Many, if not most, educators agree that parents *should* have a say in school councils, policy development, and other school issues. Here, a teacher explains:

> Unless you have people on the board and in decision-making positions, which already are very much in tune with the community, they are the experts in their cultures and their sensitivities in terms of policies. You can't come in and just decide what you think is politically correct and do it; you should be talking to the people who are affected and letting them have a say. (R3T2)

On the other hand, there is resistance to parental involvement. Although there is teacher resistance, the speakers share an inability to identify themselves or the school system as playing a part in the social relations with parents from racial and ethnic groups:

> Because you can make all the mistakes you want here and that's one of the luxuries of bringing a first year teacher up here. You don't have parents that are looking over your back and challenging you. (R3T2)

> I have mentioned those kinds of things [the Canadian educational system as different from that in other countries] in parent-teacher interviews. Again, you feel their minds are closed. You can't really tell if you're getting through or not. (R5T5)

When asked what role racial and ethnic communities should play in policy development, one teacher answers: "Oh man, how much are they prepared to?" (R1T1). In a later comment, she explains her willingness to blame marginalized groups themselves for the problem of exclusion. Efforts to solicit input from the area's black community with the purpose of revising the school's curriculum are, for this teacher, "not a major concern."

Some teachers struggle against their colleagues' resistance to parental and community involvement:

> A lot of people told that parents wouldn't be helpful, don't care, all that kind of stuff and I haven't found that to be true at all… I find the parents to be very, very concerned for the children's progress, trying their very best under very difficult circumstances. You know, limited education themselves, limited time with their children and a lot of other problems going on, so I think they really care. (R1T7)

The relationship of the school to parents, particularly to parents of racial and ethnic minorities, continues to be a problematic one. Recall the anticipation of backlash from dominant group members and the obstacles of inaccessibility, caution, or lack of awareness. Recall, as well, the presentation of the "different" that is often reserved for community participants. Educators exploit the private/public boundary that separates them from parents to justify their failed efforts in welcoming parents in an equitable manner.

The consequence of limited communication between parent and teacher contradicts a central intent of equity and diversity education—to empower traditionally marginalized communities so they may introduce change to our social institutions.

PERSPECTIVES ON PROFESSIONAL DEVELOPMENT

How do teachers perceive professional development programs that prepare them to meet the challenges of race and ethnocultural diversity within schools? The qualitative data reveal a concerted need for more professional development (PD) in MCE and ARE. Teachers perceive PD initiatives across boards to range from non-existent to sporadic. There has been little sustained, coordinated effort at the school and the board levels. The response that PD on MCE/ARE was generally non-existent is commonplace across the boards studied. The following sentiments reflect the general impression:

> I'm sure it's been available. I'm just thinking of the professional development booklet. It seems like there are a couple of things in there but I can't remember what. (R2T2)

> Maybe it has been on one of those memos, I don't know. I don't think it was clear to me that there was much available to me outside my own seeking for it. (R1T2)

Even when workshops are offered on PD days, teachers criticize limitations in the presentation:

> The missing link for our teachers I believe is showing them how anti-racism can be integrated into the curriculum. The material selection is critical and having it available is what is important. We don't have to have for example, Black History Month; it does not have to have parades, but we have to have history curriculum. So it should be inclusionary rather than exclusionary. (R3PE)

Educators' own suggestions for programs that implement MCE and ARE predictably reflect the extent to which the educators have analyzed their implications. One principal argues that some teachers are at the pre-awareness stage and lack any knowledge about the race and ethnocultural diversity of the larger community. PD content is therefore dependent on teachers' awareness level, a conclusion drawn by some race relations advisors. If MCE and ARE are understood as nothing more than a discrete set of curriculum guidelines, that explains why many research participants suggest pragmatic requirements to increase their competence. These include such things as specific information about the way in which MCE and ARE may be applied to the teacher's own area of expertise, or more time to acquire familiarity with the approach, but most often an increase in quantity of curriculum materials. One elementary school teacher describes her specific needs in this area:

> Let's say if I want to teach about Inuits [sic] because it's a part of the curriculum, we can have assigned a [curriculum] kit, which is called Inuits. Inside I have a lot of beautiful books and pictures and specimens of art and stuff like this and movies. And I wish that the Board would make those kits regarding different nationalities and different cultures. (R1T4)

Teachers express the need for content in three areas: race and ethnospecific information, classroom and school programs, and teacher competence development. First, knowledge of racial, ethnic or cultural group characteristics is sought, specifically material on: learning styles of different cultural groups, black issues, black literature, artifacts, and musical instruments, and differences and similarities among minority groups.

The need for presumably "objective" information about groups varies among educators. Provision of such information is necessary to bridge the gap between the theory of MCE/ARE and its implementation, especially when integration with other teaching areas is expected. Practical advice satisfies the need for "a quick and easy way to do this, here's a book list, concrete materials that you can take home, something you can bring to class tomorrow," explains one principal. PD programs were often criticized for failing to deliver information geared to the individual school and individual teachers' subject and grade level.

Second, respondents identify additional, more general pedagogical needs regarding PD on equity and diversity education. These focus on classroom and school programs, materials, and ideas, and include: conflict management and mediation; cooperative learning; integrating MCE/ARE approaches into each activity of schooling, and making explicit the message of cooperation in diversity.

With respect to how teachers evaluate existing PD programs they've experienced, only 33% of survey respondents agree or strongly agree that in-service training is achieving its goal of providing awareness, knowledge and skills to work effectively in MCE and ARE. Forty percent are ambivalent about the achievement of in-service goals; 27% are unimpressed by the effectiveness of in-service training in building competence in teachers.

Widespread negative evaluations about the inability of PD to affect real change is a theme in Ouseley's (1992) and Sleeter's (1992a) research as well, indicating the need to further explore the effectiveness of in-service programs. While there is a demand for the practical in PD, teachers also ask for more abstract materials on related social issues and on attitudinal change, reflection, and integration of equity and diversity into personal frameworks.

Still, resistance to PD and equity issues is common. MCE/ARE advisors who are instrumental in offering PD to teachers report their frustration:

> Part of my own frustration comes from the resistance that's often shown by teachers. The moment PD is announced, they take it to be another of those [anti-racist] events. So they see it as onerous even to attend the PD session, much less willingness to change. (R2A1)

The following teacher talks about the School Board's approach to PD as the root of cynicism:

> Pro D [professional development] in this district, I don't know whether other districts have been checked out; they will now all do this, then we will all do that and then it becomes fashionable to do a certain thing. So teachers become quite cynical and hardened to professional development. (R5T4)

There are some positive reports of PD programs, however. One particularly progressive administrator invited speakers to address his staff. Other positive experiences with PD for equity and diversity education are described below:

> He has really been trying to open people's minds; he brought in a former black graduate [sic]. He's now an architect and he came in to tell what

type of teachers influenced him and what kinds of things happened in his life to illustrate the prejudice that's still there. There was a Canadian Native person that came in and told about some of his work in trying to build identity of Native People here in the city. And a man that works with a lot of immigrants came in and told something about the immigration policy and what it's like to be deported. (R2T4)

We had three [kids] talk to the entire staff, gave their experiences, their sense of how their schooling is different from their country [of origin] and implications of what they've experienced, what they've experienced in the classroom... . Very powerful! Extremely moving. (R5T7)

The common element in both excerpts is teachers' direct encounters with members of marginalized groups. The knowledge these speakers bring as "insiders" of a racially or ethnically defined minority group carries considerable credibility. Their stories are compelling for a great many teachers who may otherwise derive from PD only that which corresponds to their own limited understanding of other cultures.

Accommodation to, even enthusiasm for PD about MCE and ARE was reported by some participants. In one board, sessions both during school hours and after-school were so oversubscribed—albeit by perhaps 20% of all staff—that the organizer had to add another day of meetings. Here one teacher describes his experience:

I've never felt I was a racial [sic] person. I've never felt that I came from a racist society. I felt Canada was pretty free of that kind of thing. The Racial Awareness workshops that [my Board] put on changed my opinion a great deal... . I was absolutely blown away by it. (R2T6)

PD initiatives that deal with topics such as stereotyping in ethnic communities and racial and ethnic group differences heighten teachers' awareness and sensitivity toward issues of MCE and ARE. Yet the manner in which PD is delivered is crucial. In our study, teachers reported a preference for more interactive, participatory approaches rather than passive lecture-style formats. Interview participants made many direct and indirect suggestions for the way in which PD on MCE and ARE ought to be conducted.

Effective PD organizers must be sensitive not only to the explicitly identified needs of participants but also to the submerged needs that arise from their values and political or ideological beliefs. Sleeter (1992a) recommends that any PD on equity and diversity education must acknowledge the established worldviews of the participants. These factors are integral to the way in which educators interpret race and ethnicity, educational inequality, and the need for equity and diversity education. More specifically, they determine how participants will interpret what they hear in a PD program and the nature of their resistance or accommodation. The success of any PD initiative is perhaps more contingent upon what participants bring to the session than anything brought by the leader.

Professional development is not restricted to in-service programs for established teachers. According to our research participants, pre-service education for prospective teachers is a most appropriate place to instill values and skills congruent with equity and diversity education. It also turns out to be an object of criticism for teachers. Many of them hold Faculties of Education responsible for their own lack of fluency in equity and diversity education. Indeed, several MCE/ARE advisors provide a version of the belief that "the root of the problem is right at the Faculties of Education." Teachers, principals, and MCE/ARE advisors in our study express concern about the inadequacy of pre-service teacher education programs for a changing society. Here are two samples of this perspective:

> Student preparation for teaching needs to acknowledge that we do not have a white, mainstream population; we have a significant percentage of "others" in the schools. We cannot teach to the mainstream population any more, it's as simple as that. And teachers who attempt to, are going to find that there's not going to be a place for them in the system, if that's the only way they are able to teach... . Those coming in better have a cross-cultural background or there's not going to be a place for them in the system. (R1A1)

> I don't think the education system at [my university] really prepares me well enough to develop a multicultural pedagogy that can help the students learn. And so, I know I'm very weak in that area and I just don't feel I've gotten enough support in my preparation... . I can cope, but you know, I could be doing better. I don't think training has us all excel in that area. (R5T2)

Just as for in-service PD on equity issues, teachers make many practical suggestions for improving pre-service education in an environment of diversity. For one, Faculties should include in their curriculum the history and the contributions of various racial, ethnic, and cultural groups. An administrator suggests, as an example, that teacher candidates be exposed to a revisionist perspective of Canadian history. Here he explains why:

> Coming from Québec, I was raised to believe that missionaries saved the Native Peoples and I know today that those missionaries destroyed Native Peoples. This needs to be looked at. Canada was not a land of liberty for black people. These things need to be discussed, the fact that our first Prime Minister had slaves... You would be amazed to know how many kids in the school believe the Japanese were interned because they were spies... The interpretation of history is very important... . This should happen at the university level, because once you hit the school, there wouldn't be time. (R4PE)

Other areas of study recommended by educators include cross-cultural and racism awareness training, courses that deal with Canada's new social fabric and its diversity of religion and culture, especially as it relates to the local community. Moreover, teachers need to know how to integrate equity and diversity education into the existing school curriculum, especially in subject areas such as mathematics and science.

Of particular challenge to prospective teachers is dealing with and integrating different cultural values into every facet of the schooling experience. Here one teacher describes her personal vision of what is required for pre-service teacher education:

> All teacher education should have a multicultural component that includes curriculum strategies and theory. It should be compulsory for all teachers who are working in this part of the world. Teachers who work with new immigrants should be trained in advocacy because they can be the most powerful advocates for these children... (R5T1)

Another respondent ponders the issue of developing attitudes toward other cultures, and speculates whether teacher education can reverse twenty to thirty years of preconceptions and stereotypes about minority groups. "It's very hard to change someone's attitude, so what can they [Faculties of Education] do exactly? I suppose they can catch people who don't have an attitude and hope that they won't develop an attitude."

For others, Faculties can do more than tackle conservative political attitudes. Some suggest that they emphasize the denial of inequity and discrimination against minorities, and the consequences these positions have on children and on teachers' performance:

> I think we can change the attitudes of people who don't see prejudices as a problem because those people, myself included, haven't had to deal with it that much, so they don't believe that it exists. You can make them aware. You can put it in their face and say, "This is happening," and I think those people will certainly step back and say, "Wow, I didn't realize that; we should do something about this to change it." (R1T7)

The role of teacher as "agent of change" is regarded as an appropriate topic for pre-service programs. One advisor suggests encouraging candidates to "make a difference" by drawing on the rich diversity to which the teacher has direct access. As part of their practicum experience, teacher candidates should be exposed to the real world of racial and cultural diversity in the school and community. To achieve this, Faculties of Education need to transform their curriculum and pedagogy.

chapter four

From Resistance to Transformative Possibilities

DECONSTRUCTING RESISTANCE

Administrators and teachers alike may engage in activities that signal commitment to equity and diversity education, but resist problematizing the racial tensions that are occurring on their doorsteps. It is difficult to identify individuals who have an affinity for issues of equity and diversity, or for whom PD has a lasting effect. Appearances may be deceiving, according to one advisor; "because people are very skilled in covering up their own feelings: they are able to camouflage those feelings and project an image that is not really their truth" (R1A1).

The underlying outward behaviour that this advisor highlights introduces a new set of questions about resistance to equity and diversity education. Legitimate claims of curricular overload notwithstanding, we have to begin to query what lies behind traditional pedagogical concerns. We are compelled to follow through on problems of indifference, ignorance, and dismissal of equity and diversity education as incompatible with what many teachers believe they ought to be doing. Even the condition of curricular overload may be contextualized further.

When asked about the connection between teacher resistance and "entrenched views of different races," one teacher responds, "I think this comes out in [the excuse that] 'I'm too busy.' People who have these entrenched views respond as though they are really busy. It's a cop-out for anything new, especially this kind of [MCE and ARE] stuff." This assertion leads to our observation that curricular overload may be one manifestation of resistance to MCE and ARE. Indeed, the balance of this chapter elaborates on the problem of resistance and then shifts to the question of transformative possibilities. It exposes many reasons why teachers resist equity and diversity education "due to curricular overload" —most complaints of which are upheld without a full appreciation of their significance.

Accommodation and resistance to MCE and ARE act as indicators of the depth of an educator's perspective on these educational reforms, as well as of his or her sincerity in engaging them as fully as possible. Studying the data leaves two general impressions. First, equity and diversity education is something that commands wide acceptance as part of teachers' overall moral code; the breadth of this acceptance is reflected by the very high level of agreement in principle with the goals of MCE and ARE as reported in Table 3.1. Second, its implications are distant from teachers' day-to-day planning, which is reflected in Table 4.1 by a lower level of support in accommodative teaching practices. The percentage differential between teachers' stated support of the principles and goals of MCE and ARE, and their day-to-day planning in order to implement these goals already shows a disconnect between stated beliefs and practices.

Our research shows, in addition to these self-reports, serious discontinuities between stated beliefs and actual practices. Forms and manifestations of resistance to MCE and ARE far outnumber forms and manifestations of accommodation. Educators often continue on in a generally traditional fashion in the classroom *in spite of their reports that they believe in doing otherwise.*

To be fair, many educators have integrated aspects of these educational innovations into their practice. But this integration, from the point of view of the MCE or ARE advocate, is piecemeal. Diversions into "other" literatures and student backgrounds are taken. Efforts at revising the "hidden" aspects of teacher expectations, evaluations, labelling, and student groupings are made. New books are selected for the classroom library; global appreciation is encouraged in social studies. Inappropriate responses to social differences are suppressed when evaluating schoolwork, and administrators' initiatives in revising the features of school events are supported. Teachers sometimes talk of student empowerment, but their practice is not likely to consistently reflect that value in a way that coextends to thorough, systematic, and institutional change toward equitable practices, treatment and outcomes for all students.

Simply describing resistance and accommodation to MCE and ARE cannot explain why their balance is so severely tipped in favor of the former. Yet in asking why this is so, our description of teacher culture must grow to include educators' interpretive framework. Their beliefs represent their personal investments in seeing and reacting to MCE and ARE educational reforms the way they do. They involve the underlying values and assumptions informing their perspectives and approaches to MCE and ARE.

Table 4.1
Teachers' Responses to a Range of MCE/ARE Teaching Practices

Valid percent

Item	Agree/ Strongly Agree	Disagree/ Strongly Disagree	Ambivalent	n
My approach to MCE is to enrich my curriculum with units about racially and ethnically diverse groups.	56.9	13.0	24.3	944
I teach that racial and ethnic diversity in the classroom is desirable.	73.3	3.8	17.6	951
I provide ways for students of diverse racial and ethnic groups to connect their lives and personal experiences to classroom topics.	73.6	4.4	19.1	974
It is important to empower students to become activists in working for social justice in their school and community.	74.7	8.7	14.7	984

Determining why educators respond the way they do reveals something about what they bring to the educational endeavour. An educator selects responses from a dynamic panorama of possibilities based on what makes sense to him or her. This choice is contingent upon establishing a close 'fit' with his or her interpretive framework and its associated values and investments. Internal inconsistencies are inevitable. The real problem with any particular pattern of selection arises, however, when there is incomplete awareness of its ultimate consequences for others.

Resistance to MCE and ARE may be placed in a context of personal commitments to ideological or political positions antagonistic to the goal of empowerment for groups marginalized on the basis of race and ethnicity. Generally, educators understand neither the links to the ideological and political strata from which traditional pedagogical concerns are derived, nor the effects they have upon minority students. A closer investigation of these links and effects lies at the heart of understanding resistance to MCE and ARE.

One teacher expresses this concern in her remarks that colleagues "think everything has been solved. And I think the big thing is they have not dealt with it themselves. They have not really looked at their thoughts and beliefs" (R1T3). "I think teachers are frightened of their own beliefs," says another, "and so they are nervous of what kids might bring up" (R1T7).

There are a few participants who are exceptions in failing to regard personal frames of reference as problematic. One of these exceptions follows:

> Being aware of other cultures and learning things about their belief systems is great. But if you already—and most us do—have a pretty set notion that your culture is better, your white culture, say, and that other people aren't as smart as you, then I think you have to deal with that first. (R1T3)

Contextualizing teachers' traditional pedagogical concerns through elaborating their ideological and political frameworks helps to explain insidious forms of educational inequity. Moreover, it ultimately provides the insight that is essential for their transformation. First, however, we must notice how teachers show resistance. This process reflects the ways in which politically and ideologically informed values emerge in a set of behaviours.

Advisors may occupy a professional and personal vantage point from which to contextualize the existence of resistance to MCE and ARE. One advisor has special insight into the phenomenon of resistance that is worth quoting at length:

> Blatant resistance is obvious by the way people talk, their tone and the content of what they say... even though the group [under discussion] might not be in that building [where] they are being talked about by the white community. They talk in tones and a manner that is not necessarily the most positive. So the subtle ones are much more difficult to detect. And it is easy for those people with subtle attitudes to cover up if they are not forced to internalize those things and respond to things as they happen. So if they are able to give almost like a yes or no answer they are able to keep their true feelings covered; but if they have to do something like respond to a situation as it occurs, their internal beliefs come forth very quickly either by the comments that they make or the decision that they make or don't make. Their response to the parents or to the community from which students come, or the classism issue, the economic situation is very telling. Those are comments that people make that I think can be subtle, but it is obvious that it delivers a

message to young people or to adults. And it comes in many forms—they won't cooperate, they put barriers in the way, they try to ensure whatever you are attempting to do is not going to be easily done, or they will try to slow you down. (R1A1)

Another advisor describes an experience of teacher resistance to MCE and ARE (also see Table 4.2 for survey findings, below):

We hear all kinds of comments, "Why do we have to do things their way?" " Why don't they go back to where they come from?" "If I went to their country they wouldn't do this for me. Why do they expect it from me?" "Why do we have to keep pandering to the needs of the ethnics or racial minorities?" "They're taking our jobs and they're taking away our traditions; They're taking us over." (R2A1)

Table 4.2
Teachers' Beliefs about Multicultural and Anti-racist Education

Valid percent

Item	Agree/ Strongly Agree	Disagree/ Strongly Disagree	Ambivalent	n
Multiculturalism and anti-racism alienate the dominant (white) groups in society.	22.1	54.2	19.5	961
MCE and ARE usually result in "reverse discrimination."	20.3	44.0	30.8	957

One politically-linked tethered reason for resistance to equity and diversity education is the belief that assimilation is the true purpose of schools and the appropriate goal for school clientele (Foster 1990; Jeevanantham 2001). Other reasons include the analysis of student failure as an exclusively individual problem (Sleeter 1992b). Teachers who report feeling uncomfortable with the 'racial anger' stirred up in PD sessions on equity and diversity education characterize claims of injustice and inequity as exaggerations. (Foster 1990)

Found between the lines of most, if not all, studies of teacher resistance is a climate lacking in empathy for or outrage against social injustice (Ahlquist

1992; Berlak 1989). Helplessness (Sleeter 1992b), powerlessness (Thomas 1986) and guilt (Ahlquist 1992) are common responses that act as additional barriers to effective implementation of equity and diversity education programs and policies. Reluctance to name the problems of racism and ethnocentrism (Mock and Masemann 1990) remains a most tenacious obstacle. This denial thrives at a sub-textual level through each of these categories of experience.

Subtle manifestations of resistance to equity and diversity education are difficult to discern because of their very function and the intent they obscure. It is essential to attend to such manifestations nonetheless. They lead to a closer inspection of resistance as it is lived, constructed, and made sense of by school agents.

Synchronized with political and ideological frameworks, manifestations of resistance contain implicit messages about how teachers explain social differences and educational disparities among schoolchildren. Locating the source of inequity with parents, with working class life, with poverty, or with society at large, in short, anywhere but within the social structure of the school itself, is a typical manifestation of resistance—the consequence of which ironically and often tragically defeats the very purpose of public education. School agents are compelled to identify a wide variety of "problems" imputed to equity and diversity education that justify their unwillingness to undertake any of its particular ideas in the classroom. The lack of support for further inquiry is buttressed by a prevailing educational ideology and political climate that is essentially conservative.

TRANSFORMATIVE POSSIBILITIES

In proceeding from resistance to equity and diversity education to transformative possibilities, we encounter a dilemma. Throughout Part I, we have presented evidence of teachers' resistance to equity and diversity education that moved well beyond individual attitudes and beliefs. We uncovered ideological and political undercurrents that effectively demonstrated the systemic nature of resistance whether it emerges in response to educational policy, practice, or professional development.

Still, it is incumbent upon us as advocates of equity and diversity to propose a workable solution to the problem of resistance that may be adapted to teachers' present conditions. We need to create direct links between academic research on equity and diversity, educational policy, and positive changes in teachers' and children's lives. The broader arena of systemic change remains abstract, inaccessible from within current professional situations, and, unfortunately, overwhelming in scope.

For now, transformation must occur on the level of professional development, as discouraging as that has been. It is a testament to our faith in the educational project that we continue to identify PD at the pre-service and in-service levels as the appropriate place to begin that transformation. When conceptualized as an ongoing, ambitious project that is accountable to the public interest in social justice, PD is capable of encompassing the implications and lessons of broad, indeed systemic change. What this would involve forms the substance of this chapter.

The data on PD for equity and diversity education catalogues the obstacles faced by in-service PD—lack of sustained time, competing interests, the logistics of organizing systemwide initiatives, and an unwillingness to challenge the status quo. Faculties of Education pre-service programs seem less constrained by such obstacles and are better positioned to mobilize transformation.

Our focus in Part II is on pre-service education, that is, on Faculties of Education aimed at the preparation of prospective teachers prior to their employment in the schools. We arrived at this emphasis as a direct result of our study. There is a widespread ineffectiveness in in-service professional development programs for equity and diversity, that is, those presented to established teachers (Cabello and Burstein 1995; Sleeter 1992a). We believe that professional development efforts are more effectively spent on the formal preparatory period.

The literature on pre-service teacher education and equity and diversity education indicates that teacher candidates present many of the same problematic responses as their veteran counterparts (Grant and Secada 1990; McDiarmid 1992; Rothenberg 1997). However, there is justification for emphasizing a focus on the pre-service foundation of professional socialization as the best, and unfortunately in many cases the only, opportunity to educate teachers for equity and diversity. Institutions of higher learning have the structure and intellectual resources with which to develop and put in place the conceptual framework necessary to effect individual and institutional change.

Change affecting the policies and practices of multiple institutions requires alliance building. These initiatives must be an integral part of the structure of a Faculty of Education. The preconditions for a social-reconstructionist (Ornstein and Levine 1989) PD agenda must be a faculty that is politically progressive and equity-conscious. Committed to moving PD for equity and diversity education well beyond a set of discrete and utilitarian prescriptions, such a faculty will not be satisfied to tinker at the fringes of institutional structures and leave unaltered the main fabric of systems that continue to reproduce themselves. We need a faculty that will guide prospective teachers to a self-examination of how their socialization has affected their participation in a society profoundly shaped by inequality. Explanations of educational inequity should receive special consideration because the confusion and inconsistency around this matter serves as a key to the whole problem of how teachers rationalize their resistance to change. It is a crucial starting point in preparing teachers to teach in a multicultural, multiracial society.

In addition, the process of selection of teacher candidates committed to equity and diversity is critical. Those with entrenched ideological positions about racial and ethnic minorities might not avail themselves of any "new" knowledge that challenges their perspective. As North America becomes increasingly multicultural and multiracial, Faculties of Education can no longer afford to train and certify teachers who, intentionally or unintentionally, maintain and reproduce the traditional social order.

Before asking "what" or "how" transformation in pre-service programs could come about, a reformulation of the "why" of teacher education is required. If schooling is an embodiment of a potential future, it is incumbent upon educators to re-qualify what kind of future it is we are trying to work toward. In this book, we advocate what Giroux (1992) calls a "critical democracy." If educators were to realize that they are intimately connected to public life, and they are responsible for fostering "democratic living", they are then recast as community participants "whose function it is to establish public spaces where students can debate, appropriate, and learn the knowledge and skills necessary to live in a critical democracy" (Giroux 1988, 201).

We must educate for a critical democracy in which all voices are equally represented. That the school system has a role in producing a critically engaged citizenship should be an integral part of teacher education programs revised to become more responsive to an increasingly pluralistic world. This world should not be conceptualized as a homogenization of interests but of "communities and collaborations without consensus." A Faculty of Education should fully integrate this vision of social difference into the mainstream curriculum. Miller (1993) argues:

> Instead of promoting educational communities and identities that promise unity and sameness, where we all will become "reflective practitioners" or cheerful "teacher-researchers," for example, what might we do to shape communities and forms of collaboration in which we could struggle together to create versions of curriculum, teaching, and learning that do not posit particular voices and experiences as representative of us all? (249)

The "struggling together" to which Miller refers highlights an important point in moving from resistance to transformation. Part of our ideological inheritance that militates against equity and diversity is the tradition of individualism. In Western cultures, the individual is assigned ultimate responsibility for the instigation and consequence of action. Rewards and status accrue to demonstrations of outstanding individual effort, often defined explicitly in terms of its independence from external conditions or group affinities. We have seen manifestations of individualism in the reasoning of many teachers in this study. Yet we would argue that reducing all meaningful action to the behaviour of individuals conflicts with collective social action.

Splintering political or educational interests into many individual units undermines the possibilities for defining collective objectives that may enhance the life chances for groups of disenfranchised people. Individualism only benefits those who enjoy the power and privilege of claiming personal success divorced from group membership. Ties to culture, history, social structures and the like are imperceptible if individual circumstances permit. In cases in which race and ethnicity permeate personal circumstances, individuals cannot extricate themselves from their collective identities.

In a critical democracy, collective interests are the building blocks of a new society. Therefore, the Western propensity to focus on individualism often leads to both a de-politicization of the very real effects of racism as well as a denial of the collectivist action necessary to make meaningful systemic changes.

The antagonism observed toward "special interest groups" is a manufactured outcome of the ideological and political contexts of privilege. Yet teachers who accommodate equity and diversity education are isolated by their blind faith in individualism. They need to locate and unite with each other and groups of others who share their outlook.

The interests of equity education advocates, racially- and ethnically-defined groups, and teachers who desire to practice equity and diversity education actually coalesce. If the efforts of these groups were integrated through dialogue, purposeful social action could result, erecting a formidable challenge to the conservative status quo. Identifying and forming alliances among groups with shared political interests is a chief instrument in establishing a shared vision of change.

How might educators and those who advise them go about transforming their practice? A view of the larger social context must be brought to bear upon teacher education, both the pre-service and in-service facilities (Dei and Calliste 2000; Levine-Rasky 1998; Ross and Smith 1992). To develop what

Wood (1985) calls a "critical literacy" toward full democratic participation (that is, the ability to recognize and criticize political and economic structures that oppress marginalized groups) teachers must develop the analytic tools with which to critique schooling, society, and self. This involves an investigation of the nature of social relations in a racially and ethnically stratified society such as ours. Open discussion of ideological and sociopolitical realities, of personal experiences, and of the tensions between these dynamics, while disturbing, is ultimately transformational. Equity and diversity education implies fundamental social change that can only take place if participants have an adequate understanding of how society works and how various social structures are mutually contingent upon one another within relations of power.

TEACHER DEVELOPMENT STRATEGIES

Professional development for equity and diversity education should include the study of education in its social context. First, it should:

- study society and schooling as arenas of conflict in which social relations are mediated by race, ethnicity, and other constructions of social difference;
- analyze the interaction of social, political, and economic structures that oppress marginalized groups;
- link "hidden" curricular issues such as means of discipline, teacher expectations and judgments about parents to the broader dynamics of inter-group power relations;
- link civic responsibility, moral accountability, enhanced political sensibility, and a commitment to work on equity issues.

Second, it should also examine all facets of the formal and "hidden" curriculum which must be scrutinized under the light of a burgeoning awareness of social issues. Ginsburg explains that "this would entail instructors and students identifying and discussing what messages are evidenced, and those which are not evidenced or are only part of the taken-for-granted background, in a given reading, handout, school/community observation" (1988, 212). The instructor's perspective and actions must be subject to critical inquiry and reflection. This in itself could comprise the experiential opportunity required for students to become committed to teach for social change in order to "evaluate the ideological influences that shape their thinking about schooling, society, themselves, and diverse others" (King 1991, 143).

Teaching for Equity and Diversity

Professional development for equity and diversity education should critically examine all curricular practices. It should:

- scrutinize explicit and implicit ideas encountered in the process of education, evaluating their ideological influences, their political interests and how these ideas interact with teachers' interpretive frameworks;
- provide practical information, resources, and guidance on how equity and diversity education may be integrated into regular classroom activities and how these may be revised to correspond more closely with the objectives of equity and diversity education;
- provide the opportunity for the application of equity and diversity education to the classroom through judicious practicum placements for pre-service teachers;
- provide the opportunity for veteran host teachers to participate in re-skilling and re-professionalizing activities alongside pre-service teachers.

Third, issues of "ethnicity" and "race" must be integrated into the mainstream dialogues of teacher education (Gollnick 1992; Nevarez, Sanford and Parker 1997). These issues, while fundamental to capitalist, patriarchal, racially-stratified societies such as that of North America are managed in ways that are replete with contradictions. Educators need opportunities to become conscious of oppression by "advantaging the least advantaged" in their studies (Connell 1992; McCarthy 1990). The point is not to create ghettos of special topics serving diverse groups but to reconstruct the mainstream practice as truly pluralistic. Moreover, it is essential that difference be regarded as a political category, not an objective or scientific one. We now know that the human race is a biological singularity.

Such factors as social and economic exploitation, political disenfranchisement and cultural and ideological repression have produced different racial categories that vary with time and place. Racism is no longer understood only as the consequence of historical systems of inequity. It is more accurate to regard racism as a way in which contemporary social relations are organized. Race is integral to our present ways of structuring our everyday social interactions, our language, and our social institutions.

Professional development for equity and diversity education should integrate the study of social difference, race, and anti-racism into the mainstream of teacher education scholarship. It should:

- provide historical information about racial and ethnic minority groups to correct stereotypes and misinformation;
- understand the social significance of race and the "deconstructing" of its conventional meaning;
- define racism from the point of view of those who experience it in their everyday lives and, theoretically, as a way of structuring all our lives;
- provide a stable conceptualization of anti-racism pedagogy that integrates the structural dynamics and subjective dimensions of exclusion on which solid classroom practice may be built;
- provide a clear definition of equity and diversity education and its relations to other forms of sociopolitical movements;
- develop a clear rationale for equity and diversity education including persuasive data on educational inequities for groups discriminated against on the basis of race, ethnicity, social class, first language, culture, and more;
- link the marginalization and oppression of ethnic, social class, gender, language, and religious groups to a capitalist, patriarchal, racially stratified North American structure.

Fourth, teacher education must be committed to the cause of social justice defined as those "active efforts for structural change undertaken by and on behalf of those communities which have been and remain marginalized by, and excluded from socio-cultural, economic and political power" (Toms and Scarr 1993, 2-3). Education is inextricably related to the social order, and movement on one front must complement any change on the other. McCarthy (1990) points to the necessity of amalgamating structuralist concerns with the state, labour, economy, industry, immigration policy, selective budget expenditures, trade, and the like with culturalist concerns such as that of identity, meaning-construction, everyday practices, interactions between actors, curriculum, classroom practices, teacher expectations, and equity of treatment and outcome (also see Giroux 1992, ch. 5).

As an example, McCarthy wants to unite inquiries of individual achievement and minority representation in the curriculum with problems of jobs, immigration policies and child care for minority working parents. This is one way of merging initiatives for anti-racism reform in education with wider struggles for change in existing class and gender relations in a capitalist society. In addition, reformist policies concerning changes at a particular school should encompass inquiries into local conditions of unemployment, housing conditions, competition, and declining social services (Troyna and Williams 1986, 106). Concerns about the effects of streaming, academic failure and underachievement, lower teacher expectations, and higher drop-out rates of minority students should be joined to other experiences and struggles within the society, such as the over-policing of minority neighborhoods, sexual harassment, and the marginalization of minority and majority women in the workplace, and the infrastructural needs of minority communities.

Professional development for equity and diversity education should link teacher education to social action. It should:

- develop a consciousness among teachers that moves beyond a neutral, "colour-blind" framework to a more politically informed orientation;
- draw the explicit relationship between equity education and action on social justice problems, indicating specific possibilities for classroom practice;
- focus on the political and moral dimensions of teachers' work in the development of a critical capacity to articulate a desirable future for all;
- link schooling, the social order, and issues of personal identity and professionalism in an effort to integrate "structuralist" and "culturalist" approaches to the analysis of education;
- identify other groups who share an interest in social justice, equity and diversity, and begin dialogues on forming collective projects.

The fifth and final point to make with regard to pedagogical strategies emerges from recent scholarship in what is now known as reflective practice. This approach is premised upon the idea that examination, reformulation, and testing of one's intuitive understandings is far more significant in an educator's professional development than one's technical knowledge (Schön 1983). The process of reflection should take into account one's own practices, beliefs, interpretations of difference in the classroom, one's professional role, identity, vision, and goals of the educational good. However, reflective practice should involve not only individual introspection on one's subjective orientation as a contemporary educator, but also a critical praxis of coming to terms with the complexity of the issues involved.

If Sleeter's and Grant's (1988) advice to begin with the circumstances of one's own life is to be taken seriously, directing attention toward one's personal location in a stratified society becomes a vital component of any critically reflective practice, a deliberate politicization of mainstream reflective practice. That is, educators' reflection must concern personal identities as social actors who occupy specific positions characterized by skin colour, social class, gender, religion, ethnicity, ability, and sexuality. Of particular interest here is the emerging writings on white racialization both within educational discourse (e.g., Adkins and Hytten 2000; Levine-Rasky 2000a; McIntyre 1997; Warren 1999) and beyond it (e.g., Fine, Weis, Powell and Wong 1997; Levine-Rasky 2002; Morrison 1992; Schick 2000).

The fact that "race, " as with most of these characteristics, is usually ascribed to others and not to members of the dominant groups demonstrates how it is used in society to name others and construct boundaries around groups. It obscures patterns of power differences among "marked" and "unmarked" groups. Yet Whites cannot escape their identifications with historically and culturally dominant groups. What is their role in transforming education so that it prepares its students for critical democracy?

"We in the first World" advises Welch, "are not responsible for others; we are responsible for ourselves—for seeing the limits of our own vision and for rectifying the damages caused by the arrogant violation of those limits" (1990, 139). The practice of self-reflection should be directed to personal accountability for participation in a social order permeated with social, economic, political, and historical inequities.

Professional development for equity and diversity education should develop a multi-dimensional, critical reflective practice. It should:

- critically explore issues such as emotional responses to new and dissonant knowledge forms and the myth of meritocracy for all versus the fact of privilege for some;
- develop analytic tools to disassemble preconceptions about the socially different and about white racialization and the locations these identities occupy relative to each other in political, economic, and social contexts;
- acknowledge and respect teachers' conceptions, capacities, and desires while identifying inadequacies and moving to modify and transform them;
- interrogate resistance to equity and diversity education located within teacher ideologies and subjectivities in social, political, and historical context.

It is precisely because these issues resonate with moral sensibilities that the task that lies before us is so complex. Yet we feel that perspectives and practices on equity and diversity education can be changed to accompany broad structural reform through a comprehensive and widely-framed professional development program. To consolidate our views on transformative possibilities, those running teacher education programs should investigate and adapt to their local circumstances the ideas found in this chapter that are born from this and other related research.

The lists are not intended to be exhaustive. As a point of qualification, arbitrary divisions between what are actually interdependent categories were made for clarity of presentation. More critically, practical and theoretical possibilities appear together, corresponding to our concern for the development of praxis for equity and diversity education in teacher education as the only viable route to achieving transformation. We have described enduring obstacles such as the denial of race and racism, problematic interpretations of equity and diversity education, preoccupation with traditional views on learning and teaching, and conservative views on difference and equality. We have documented persistent beliefs about assimilation, a national identity, the perceived threat to entitlement to social rewards posed by racially and ethnically defined groups, and exploited/exploiter role reversal.

Yet we maintain that a revitalized and restructured program that helps teachers to enact a transformative equity and diversity pedagogy merits a closer examination. While corresponding more closely to pre-service programs, our proposal could be adapted for in-service professional development as well. Indeed, systemwide change is far more assured if there is a simultaneous renewal of educational practices both in Faculties of Education and in practica sites in the public schools. The construction of such programs is an ongoing project inspired by the prospect of pushing the edges of all equity policies and formal ideals to their necessary linkage with social action.

part two

Research
to Practice

Part II of this book moves from the research on in-service teachers' perspectives and practices of equity and diversity to the preparation of pre-service teachers for working competently with equity and diversity in schools and communities. The context for this section is York University's Urban Diversity Teacher Education program, which was developed in 1994 as a response to the Ontario Ministry of Education's challenge (to the Faculties of Education) to make their teacher development programs more relevant to the growing diversity within the province's schools and the communities they serve.

This institutional adaptation was also a strategic response to the Faculty's Access Initiative, which targeted and recruited groups in the Ontario population that were grossly under-represented in its teaching force. Such groups included people of colour or visible minorities, Aboriginal (First Nations) Peoples, persons with disabilities, and people from refugee backgrounds. One of the objectives of the Urban Diversity Program was to create a more equitable and inclusive learning-to-teach environment. The aim was to create a faculty that was accessible and would accommodate both academically and socially the evolving diversity of teacher candidates that were being admitted through the Faculty's more equitable admissions process.

The research and analysis in Part I of this book points to a clear need for teacher education programs to reconsider how professional development is conceptualized. Thinking critically about the modern makeup of the classroom and the pedagogical and social complexities that issues of race, ethnicity and culture bring to this environment demands a thorough re-conceptualization of teacher preparation programs. What the research in Part I has made clear is that the complex issues of race, ethnicity and culture can no longer be dismissed by reductive notions of multiculturalism and diversity. An integral step in this process is the expansion of the definition and understanding of what is implied by the concept of teacher development. To this end, the Urban Diversity Teacher Education Program at York University integrates the study of race and social difference into both its curriculum and pedagogy. The program implicitly and explicitly points out that the study of race and social difference acts as an integral component in envisioning schooling as a potentially effective institution for achieving social justice. This conception of schooling for social justice is linked with broader collective action.

The broader, progressive teacher education research and practice that follows gives salience to the promotion of learning environments where teachers of diverse backgrounds are provided with extended opportunities to develop teaching competencies and professional relationships in a collaborative and interdependent manner. Such a learning environment allows these teachers to move beyond the "university wall" to form a "community of learners" in both their practicum schools and the communities they serve.

The chapters that follow will document the theoretically-informed creative adventures that ensue from moving from research to practice, as well as the many challenges along the way.

chapter five

Racial Identity Development and Teaching

RACIAL IDENTITY FORMATION AND TEACHERS

Part I of this book documents the many ways in which teachers' attitudes and perspectives on race, racism and anti-racism influence their classroom practices and their relationships with the racially "different" in the larger Canadian society. In this chapter we explore the concept of racial identity formation and examine how attitudes, beliefs, worldviews and knowledge may develop in racialized beings in racialized societies. The socializing effects of family, school, community, and media are powerful in instilling ideas about self and other. Such social formations often provide a reference point for developing preconceived notions of, and interaction with, those who are perceived to be socially different. Identity provides the lens through which people view themselves, others, and the world around them.

For a teaching force that has been socialized and educated in a society with a history of racism, one that denies white privilege and blames the victim of racism for perceived shortcomings, one that emphasizes "colour-blindness" and negates racial difference, there is need for critical self-reflection on what King (1991) labels "dysconscious racism." This is "an uncritical habit of mind that justifies inequity and exploitation by accepting the order of things as given; dysconscious racism is a form of racism that tacitly accepts dominant white norms and privileges" (135).

The objective of this chapter, therefore, is to help teachers reflect on their own racial identity development and to engage them in consciousness-raising discourses that lead to a more equitable schooling of racialized minorities, and indeed, all children. More specifically, this chapter will help teachers:

- Locate and interrogate the status of their racial identity development in terms of their awareness, attitudes, knowledge and behaviours toward racialized minorities in school and Canadian society at large;

- Develop and implement a plan of action for personal and professional growth to a level of competency and commitment to teach the racially different.

In addition, this chapter will explore some of the challenges in achieving the above objectives, provide strategies for overcoming such challenges, and discuss the implications of these challenges for teacher education.

Over the past three decades many theories and models of identity development have been explored in the research literature. Essentially, researchers and practitioners alike were trying to theorize how people come to understand themselves as racial beings in racially diverse societies, and exploring models or formulations that explain the transformation of these individuals as they interact with those who are racially different. Cross (1971) researched the various stages through which black Americans evolve at the early states from self-degradation (in terms of their position to Whites) to a position of positive, highly valued black identity and culture. Since then, theories and models of the identity development of other social groups have evolved: white racial identity (Helms 1984); Asian-American identity (Kim 1981; Kitano 1982; Lee 1991); Latina Hispanic-American identity (Ruiz 1990); Aboriginal-American identity (Choney, Berryhill-Paapke and Robbins 1995).

Essentially, these theories reject the fixed biological definition of race and claim that race is socially and psychologically constructed (Howard, 1998). The Helms' racial identity models are often used in the fields of counselling psychology and education, and are widely referenced in the academic literature.

According to Helms, the development of white people and people of colour occurs as individuals interpret and respond to the racial information in their environment. In response to this information, white people and people of colour adopt over time particular behaviours that are directly related to how they perceive themselves as socially and racially situated. These behaviours become psychologically internalized and begin to dominate the individuals' complex repertoire of behaviours. A schema or manner of behaving is defined as dominant when it is used in most situations. Helms (1995) explains, "Each time a person is exposed to or believes he or she is exposed to a racial event, the ego selects the dominant racial identity status to assist the person in interpreting the event" (187). Responding to racially-based environmental cues that occur in these situations provides the person with a sense of well-being and self-esteem.

According to the Helms' early model formulations, statuses develop or mature sequentially. The white racial identity ego statuses range from the "Contact Status" where the individual is oblivious to racism and is satisfied with the racial status quo to the "Autonomy Status" where she or he has developed a positive socio-racial group commitment and has the capacity to abandon white entitlement and the privileges of racism. The People of Colour racial identity ego statuses range from "Conformity (Pre-Encounter) Status" where the individual shows allegiances to white standards of merit at the expense of own-group abandonment, to "Integrative Awareness Status" where the individual values the collective identity. Movements among these statuses occur when an individual's dominant schema can no longer sustain a comfort level, and the person must change viewpoint in order to psychologically survive a racial situation.

The importance of racial identity development theories is the salience they give to race in inter-group interaction and relationships, and the continuous self-reflection and self-examination that allow individuals to move from an inchoate status to the more advanced status. Thompson and Carter (1997, 17) state:

> Racial identity development entails a continual and deliberate practice of self examination and experiencing... . In developing racial identity, peoples must undertake careful reflection on the extent to which racial indoctrination has influenced and continues to influence their lives and the manner in which they relate to others who are racially similar or racially dissimilar to themselves. These experiences are ongoing and lifelong.

Initially, racial identity development models have been utilized by disciplines such as psychology and counseling psychology, multicultural counseling and organizational development in the preparation of professionals for working with racial diversity. More and more however, the college curricula in the U.S. have been exposing their students to race-related content and pedagogy. Tatum's (1992) study *Talking about race, learning about racism: The application of racial identity development theory in the classroom* reveals interesting emotional and cognitive responses of college students to such a curriculum. Some of the working assumptions for her course, the Psychology of Racism, were that:

- Racism was pervasive in contemporary American society and there were personal, cultural and institutional manifestations;

- There were negative effects of prejudice on inter-group interactions, especially upon racially subordinate groups in a society where social and cultural power is predominantly in the hands of Whites;
- The system of advantage in American society clearly benefits Whites (white privilege);
- During their formative years children were not to blame for learning racism that was inherent in their environment, but as adults they "have a responsibility to interrupt the cycle of oppression" (4); and
- Change is possible; prejudice and racism can be understood and unlearned. Such unlearning can be a life-long process.

Tatum's predominantly white college students responded with guilt, shame, anger and despair to the race-related course content. She identified the following as the main sources of resistance (5):

1. Race is considered a taboo topic for discussion, especially in racially-mixed settings;
2. Many students, regardless of racial-group memberships, have been socialized to think of the United States as a just society;
3. Many students, particularly white students, initially deny any personal prejudice, recognizing the impact of racism on other people's lives, but fail to acknowledge its impact on their own (5).

Tatum's research is instructive to educators who are exploring the application of racial identity development in their classroom teaching. Here, she offers four strategies for reducing student resistance and promoting student development:

1. The creation of a safe classroom atmosphere by establishing clear guidelines for discussion;
2. The creation of opportunities for self-generated knowledge;
3. The provision of an appropriate developmental model that students can use as a framework for understanding their own process;
4. The exploration of strategies to empower students as change agents. (18)

In their developmental approach to teaching or learning anti-racism, Derman-Sparks and Phillips (1997) report that both white students and students of colour participating in their anti-racism college courses go through phases of conflict, disequilibria, transformation, and activism to achieve the course goals of anti-racist consciousness and behaviour. Significant in the application of Derman-Sparks' and Phillips' model is the finding that white students and students of colour took different pathways to achieve transformation and activism:

> While creation of a new identity requires people of colour to first break away from the dominant culture, reconnect with their own group, and then find ways to reestablish connections with the dominant culture based on a new sense of identity, Whites must first distance themselves from their own group, determine what they want to keep and discard, and then establish a new identity that enables them to maintain a dual relationship to their group—reconnecting, on one hand, and challenging its roles and racism on the other. (32)

Derman-Sparks and Phillips conclude that a solid commitment to anti-racism work requires Whites to break the silence and expose white privilege as Peggy McIntosh (1989) urged in *White privilege: Unpacking the invisible knapsack.* By the same token, people of colour are challenged to confront and resist oppression by creating alliances with others in similar situations. The significance of racial identity development for teacher education lies in the exposure of teachers' "dysconsciousness" or uncritical beliefs, attitudes and perceptions of the existing social order. It allows teachers to grow and believe in possibilities of change.

King's (1991) analysis of teachers' impaired consciousness or distorted ways of thinking about race has far reaching implications for teacher preparation in a racially-diverse school environment. She advocates a liberatory pedagogy in teacher education programs that helps candidates develop the critical skills required for teaching equitably the "racial other".

The theories of racial identity development, despite their many benefits, have some important limitations. According to Howard (1998) and Tatum (1992), Helms' (1995) white racial identity development model may be used as a guide and as an educative tool, but it might not reflect the experience of everyone. In her recent study, *The social construction of racial identity of white student teachers and its impact on their learning to teach,* Robertson-Baghel (1998) raised a number of issues, and argued that current models of racial identity development are inadequate in framing the wide variance in identity statuses and information-processing strategies of pre-service teachers. In addition, there is a tendency to essentialize race and minority groups; communities are often seen as homogeneous entities. Furthermore, such an approach to racial identity does not allow for an analysis of a more complex racial identity development in which the intersection of race with other identities such as ethnicity, gender, social class and issues of sexuality can be discussed.

In this regard, McCarthy and Crichlow (1993) advance a relational and interdisciplinary approach to the discussion of racial identity and unequal relations in schools. They contend:

> A relational and nonessential approach to the discussion of racial identities allows for a more complex understanding of the educational and political behaviour of minority groups... There is a need to move beyond static definitions of whites and blacks as they currently pervade existing research in education. (xix)

PROGRAM DESIGN AND IMPLEMENTATION

Designing a teacher education approach that explores racial identity development and its potential impact on practice, and one that prepares teachers to work competently and equitably in a racially diverse environment requires the following interventions:

- Making an initial baseline of teachers' racial identity development status; their awareness, attitudes, beliefs and knowledge about racial diversity and difference; perspectives on anti-racism education; and their current level of competency in teaching from an anti-racism perspective.
- The development of individual growth plans that will move participants from their initial status to a higher level of consciousness and competency for working with race. Such a growth plan should be achievable during the year of learning to teach.

This growth plan should have applicability in real (practicum) schools and the communities they serve.

Study Setting and Participants
To implement this racial identity study design, pre-service teachers were chosen from York's one-year, post-baccalaureate Urban Diversity Program. Specific

objectives of this primary/junior teacher education program were to integrate issues of equity, diversity and social justice into foundational courses as well as the classroom curriculum of co-operating (practicum) schools. Over 60% of the student teachers' pre-service year was spent in urban schools chosen to reflect the racial-ethnocultural diversity of the urban population. Recent demographic studies revealed that visible minorities in this urban centre constituted about 50% of the population.

A group of 36 volunteers were selected from a larger cohort of 82 pre-service teachers, to ensure equitable representation of the following social groups and practicum schools:

- Racial distribution: A fairly even number of Asians, Blacks and Whites were chosen to reflect the proportion in the larger pre-service cohort. Of the 36 volunteers, 18 identified themselves as People of Colour and fell into two distinct sub-groups: people of African and Asian heritages. Of those identifying themselves as Whites, most were of British, Jewish and Canadian[1] heritage. While most participants were Canadian born, a number of them from both groups were immigrants, schooled to varying degrees in their countries of origin before migrating to Canada. As well, there was a wide range of religious affiliation in both groups: Christianity (Catholics and Protestants), Hinduism, Islam and Judaism.
- Gender representation: The proportion of males and females in the sample reflected those in the larger cohort.
- Practicum school racial diversity: Only practicum schools with a high degree of racial or ethnic diversity in their student populations were selected for the project.

To document the implementation of this racial identity development (RID) study, we utilized both quantitative and qualitative data collection and analysis approaches over the year of teacher education:

- Early September: pre-program data collection and development of growth plans;
- Late November: first round observation and follow-up interviews in practicum schools;
- January/February: preliminary data analysis;
- May: second round observation and follow-up interviews in practicum schools;

- June: post-program evaluations and reflections.[2]

Pre-program Baselining

The following instruments were utilized to determine pre-service teachers' level of racial identity development, knowledge and awareness of diversity and perspectives on anti-racism education within schools:

- Discovering Diversity Profile (DDP): This commercially-developed instrument measured pre-service teachers' knowledge, understanding, acceptance and behaviour as key areas that influenced their response to diversity. It provided suggestions for growth in these categories.
- Racial Identity Development (RID): This instrument ascertained participants' RID status—their personal awareness, knowledge and consciousness about cross-race contact and inter-group relations. An adaptation of Helms' (1995) model is used to capture the experiences and perspectives of both Whites and People of Colour. On this chart participants identify with pre-selected items that best describe and reflect the RID status and the information processing strategies (IPS) most often used at that level. For people of colour these statuses range from lower to higher order response styles: Conformity (Pre-encounter), Dissonance (Encounter), Immersion/Emersion, Internalization, and Integrative awareness. For Whites statuses range from 1 to 6: Contact, Disintegration, Re-integration, Pseudoindependence, Immersion/Emersion, Autonomy (see Helms (1995) for the elaborated model).
- Multicultural/Anti-racism Education Survey: This survey consists of 55 statements, utilizing a 5-point Likert response scale to ascertain respondents' perspectives on various aspects of multicultural and anti-racism education policy and practice. Survey items cover such themes as general beliefs about race, ethnicity and anti-racism; teaching practices and other school practices; school-community relations; professional development for working with diversity; beliefs about racial and ethnic groups' commitment to education.
- Interview Guide, Racial Identity Development: This 10-question instrument ascertained participants' awareness of their racial identity, racial difference, the extent of racism in Canadian society, and the potential impact of teachers' racial identity on their work

in racially-diverse schools. Based on their level of awareness, participants were asked about their personal and professional needs and growth plan. Interviews were audiotaped for transcription and analysis. From these data, participants charted and established baselines for their levels of awareness and knowledge of diversity with specific focus on race. Reliable individual and group profiles resulted from these baseline data. More importantly, the profiles identified areas of need and helped participants to chart realistic plans for personal and professional growth over the year of learning to teach. Common areas of need were communicated to course directors to be addressed in their courses.

Practicum Classroom Observations and Follow-up Interviews
We scheduled observation sessions. The first was conducted during the first practicum block in November; the second was carried out in May of the following year. We conducted the sessions to determine the extent to which candidates were implementing their growth plans. We used two observation guides. The Generic Guide recorded candidates' competence level in implementing an inclusive anti-racism curriculum and interacting cross-racially. The Individualized Observation Guide documented the extent to which candidates were achieving their growth plan objectives. Follow-up interviews provided clarifying and/or additional data to the researcher's classroom observation. A school cohort focus group discussion provided the opportunity for candidates to share their teaching experiences with the researcher concerning factors facilitating or hindering the objectives of their growth plans.

Post-program Evaluations
We performed this evaluation to ascertain the extent to which pre-service teachers realized their growth plan objectives and to identify the personal, programmatic and institutional factors that facilitated or hindered growth. Anecdotal reports, journal entries, surveys, focus groups and individual interviews were used to collect these data. Interviews were audiotaped for transcription and analysis.

Analysis of Data
We used both quantitative and qualitative approaches to analyze the range of data collected. In the quantification of data from survey questionnaires,

frequency charts provided some general patterns in the data. Pre- and post-program frequency charts from survey data were analyzed and compared to determine the extent to which program intervention and other factors might have changed candidates' perspectives on race, identity and the schooling process. The interview and other qualitative data provided a deeper and more complex exploration of participants' racial identities and the ways these might impact their learning to teach.

Data collection and analysis followed a process that Glaser and Strauss (1967), Erickson (1986) and Le Compte and Preissle (1993) describe as the constant comparison method. Research team members performed analysis as an ongoing process by independently reviewing transcripts in an iterative manner.

Ongoing research team meetings provided investigators with the opportunity to participate at all levels of the data analysis phase. At the initial stages of data collection the team developed analytic files, rudimentary coding schemes and potential coding categories that enhanced the trustworthiness of the data (Stake 1995). In these regular group sessions, the researchers provided different interpretations of the data instead of simply confirming a single meaning. Because the research team members were racially diverse, they brought to the analysis varied perceptions and interpretations based on their own experiences in multiracial schools and a racialized Canadian society. This process is what Stake (1995, 115) terms "researcher triangulation." This ongoing audit of the research process helped with the generation of common themes and a working hypothesis (Lincoln and Guba, 1985, 38). In the reporting process, generalizations about the data were grounded in such specifics as quotations from individual and focus-group interviews, and observational and survey data.

Growth Needs for Racial Identity Development

From the baseline data, a number of learning needs related to participants' racial identity development emerged. Those most frequently mentioned were:

- Learning about others' racial and ethno-cultural histories and becoming receptive to other cultural ideas, perspectives and ways of knowing;
- Developing strategies to improve the acceptance of racially diverse groups;
- Understanding the shifting nature of race as a social category and its implications for teaching and learning;

- Understanding the concepts "colour-blindness" and "racelessness" (see below), their causes and consequences in teaching and learning;
- Becoming more conscious of power and privilege in the social construction of "whiteness" and racial minority status in school and society;
- Establishing a connection between the social construction of race, social class, gender, and sexual orientation as forms of oppression and addressing these inequities in an anti-racism curriculum;
- Becoming more open to discussing issues of race, and learning the "correct" language to discuss racism;
- Learning strategies to detect and deal effectively and equitably with racism in school and society;
- Working on interpersonal skills—how to communicate, deal with conflict, and cope with making mistakes in cross-race environments;
- Gaining more information about non-eurocentric curricula and seeking out relevant learning materials for an anti-racism curriculum.

Growth Plans

We found the teacher education curriculum to be instrumental in integrating into its theoretical structure and practicum courses some of the identified growth needs of participants. For example, issues of equity, social justice, and diversity were applied to the considerations of curriculum, the student body, and teaching staff. To further personalize their growth plans, participants listed such activities as: attend cultural events in ethnic communities; participate in open, frank discussions of race and racism with friends, teacher colleagues, and family members, and confront racist and ethnocentric attitudes and behaviours; make a list of racial and ethnic stereotypes and try to avoid them; explore learning materials (print, videos, audio programs) for stereotype-free information about ethnocultural groups in Canadian society and invite resource persons from ethno-racial communities to participate in the schooling process.

Each participant's growth plan was charted on an Individualized Observation Guide to document and monitor the extent to which individuals were achieving their growth plan objectives. The teacher-education structure of building collegial practicum-school cohort group culture and interdependent classroom dyad partnerships (this concept will be discussed in the next chapter) provided the opportunity for self and partner monitoring and plan implementation.

In addition, teacher educators and project research assistants conducted classroom observations and follow-up interviews to monitor and document progress. These discussions provided the opportunity for participants to share their growth experiences. From these data two salient themes emerged:

- Personal and professional growth achievement in relation to growth plans;
- Personal, institutional and programmatic obstacles to growth.

Post-Program Evidence of Participants' Growth

Post-program reflections revealed several areas of growth in awareness, knowledge and skills.

Candidates experienced growth in:

- Awareness of cultural stereotyping;
- Awareness of "whiteness" as privilege in Canadian society. Some participants developed a clearer understanding of the intersections of racial, ethnic, gender, and social class inequalities in the schooling process;
- Skills in dealing with conflict situations in school;
- Use of more inclusive language in the classroom. Such learning was aided by required and supplementary course readings, the ethnic and racial diversity of the cohort group and association with dyad partners who were racially or ethnically different;
- Understanding and theoretical grounding of the term "colour-blindness". However, some participants insisted on using the term to describe a liberal approach to race and education and to demonstrate equal treatment for all racial groups; and
- Awareness of how race mediates life. Some participants "of colour" felt more prepared to deal with this reality.

CHALLENGES OF IMPLEMENTING A RACIAL IDENTITY DEVELOPMENT PROGRAM

Participants' Responses to RID Model

This program utilized the Helms (1995) model of racial identity development to assess participants' status and to help them grow to achieve a higher status that would make them more competent teachers in racially-diverse teaching environments.

From the outset some participants had difficulty identifying themselves as either white or people of colour (these categories were a requirement for utilizing this model). For example, some Jewish, Egyptian and Iranian participants found it problematic classifying themselves as either white or persons of colour. As one Jewish participant explains:

> I don't think of myself as white, to be honest. I never think of people as white or dark coloured skin; this time [identifying racially] is the first time I'm thinking as white. If someone asks me to describe myself, I'd say, "I'm a Jewish woman."

It was clear that the interplay of racial, ethnic, cultural and national identities complicates participants' efforts to define themselves as either white or person of colour; the process of racialization in the Canadian context constructs whiteness as the norm against which social difference is determined. For example, some self-described Whites who identified as non-hyphenated Canadians and claimed fifth and sixth generation status, tended to see themselves as "raceless." One asserts:

> I don't think of white as a race. I would have to think of it as a cultural identity. I just don't think that white means anything; it has no context to me; it's like saying you are Canadian. It doesn't mean anything to me.

Many of the white candidates, who identified strongly with "racelessness," reported that they spent their formative years in homogeneous, white neighbourhoods and did not have personal experience with racial differences. These participants explained that their own racist attitudes, stereotypes, and intolerance for social groups such as Natives and Blacks, were learned through association with relatives and peers. Moreover, their responses suggest that some of these participants selectively chose from lived experiences to reinforce stereotypes:

While driving taxi you see the drug dealers who were black and you see the underbelly of society and a lot of it is black and it's really hard. Like sometimes I have to catch myself because especially with the robberies, it 'pissed' me off and expanded it [the stereotype] to the whole black community.

The narratives of the participants suggest that some of the white candidates are located at the lower end of Helms' (1995) White Racial Identity Ego Status and Information-processing Strategies. Interviews with white candidates reveal their lack of awareness of white privilege, fear of Blacks based on selective experiences, and little more than curiosity about the racial "other".

Paradoxically, these same candidates placed themselves at a high racial identity ego status (Table 5.1). Almost half of the white respondents rated themselves at the highest status: Autonomy. At this stage candidates are expected to internalise a newly defined sense of themselves as white, confront racism, and engage in an ongoing process, continually open to new information and new ways of thinking (Helms, 1995). At this early stage of their teacher education and with little or no prior exposure to anti-racist education, candidates were not ready to make an informed commitment to challenge racism in their environments.

As will be shown later, their growth plans revealed that they were, in fact, at the initial stage of acquiring ethno-specific knowledge and awareness of the ethno-cultural diversity around them. Why then did candidates engage in the practice of "status inflation" in this exercise? Commentators speculate that respondents do not want to be perceived as ignorant, intolerant or even racist, so they located themselves at "favourable" positions on the scale.

Notably, the majority of candidates of colour placed themselves at "Status 4"–Internalization (see Table 5.2). At this stage, individuals tend to feel secure in their own racial identity, and willing to establish meaningful relationships with Whites and other groups:

My best friend is from England, that is, she is White. My other good friends are of Sri Lankan, Indian, Jamaican, Hong Kong and Vietnamese backgrounds. Our little group is a very big mixture, we actually pride ourselves on that; we always say when we go out, we are the 'United Nations'.

The participants' narratives revealed that candidates' awareness of racial difference and development of a racial identity occurred at different stages in

Table 5.1
White Racial Identity Ego Statuses and
Information-Processing Strategies (IPS)*

Statuses and Strategies	*% of Teacher Candidates*
1. Contact Status: satisfaction with racial status quo, obliviousness to racism and one's participation in it. If racial factors influence life decisions, they do so in a simplistic fashion. **IPS: Obliviousness.**	0.0
2. Disintegration Status: disorientation and anxiety provoked by unresolvable racial moral dilemmas that force one to choose between own-group loyalty and humanism. May be stymied by life situations that arouse racial dilemmas. **IPS: Suppression and ambivalence.**	0.0
3. Reintegration Status: idealization of one's socio-racial group, denigration of and intolerance for other groups. Racial factors may strongly influence life decisions. **IPS: Selective perception and negative out-group distortion.**	0.0
4. Pseudo-independence Status: intellectualized commitment to one's own socio-racial group and deceptive tolerance of other groups. May make life decisions to "help" other racial groups. **IPS: Reshaping reality and selective perception.**	27.7
5. Immersion/Emersion Status: search for an understanding of the personal meaning of racism and the way by which a white person benefits from it—a redefinition of whiteness. Life choices may incorporate racial activism. **IPS: Hypervigilance and reshaping.**	16.6
6. Autonomy Status: informed positive socio-racial-group commitment, use of internal standards for self-definition, capacity to relinquish the privileges of racism. May avoid life options that require participation in racial oppression. **IPS: Flexibility and complexity.**	44.4
No Response	11.0
No. of participants: 18	100.0

* An adaptation of Helms' (1995) White and people of colour racial identity models. In J. Ponterotto, J.M. Casas, L.A. Suzuki, and C.M. Alexander, ed. *Handbook of Multicultural Counseling*. Thousand Oaks, CA: Sage.

Table 5.2
People of Colour Racial Identity Ego Statuses and Information-Processing Strategies (IPS)*

Statuses and Strategies	*% of Teacher Candidates*
1. Conformity (Pre-Encounter) Status: external self-definition that implies devaluing of own group and allegiance to White standards of merit. Probably is oblivious to socio-racial groups' sociopolitical histories. **IPS: Selective perception and obliviousness to socio-racial concerns.**	0.0
2. Dissonance (Encounter) Status: ambivalence and confusion concerning own socio-racial group commitment and ambivalent socio-racial self-definition. May be ambivalent about life decisions. **IPS: Repression of anxiety-provoking racial information.**	5.5
3. Immersion/Emersion Status: Idealization of one's group and denigration of that which is perceived as White. Use of own-group external standard to self-define, and own-group commitment and loyalty is valued. May make life decisions for the benefit of the group. **IPS: Hypervigilance toward racial stimuli and dichotomous thinking.**	11.0
4. Internalization Status: positive commitment to one's own socio-racial group. Internally defined racial attributes, and capacity to assess and respond objectively to members of the dominant group. Can make life decisions by assessing and integrating socio-racial group requirements and self-assessment. **IPS: Flexibility and analytic thinking.**	72.5
5. Integrative Awareness Status: capacity to value one's own collective identities as well as empathize and collaborate with members of other oppressed groups. Life decisions may be motivated by globally humanistic self-expression. **IPS: Flexibility and complexity.**	11.0
No. of participants:18	100.0

* An adaptation of Helms' (1995) White and people of colour racial identity models. In J. Ponterotto, J.M. Casas, L.A. Suzuki, and C.M. Alexander, ed. *Handbook of Multicultural Counseling*. Thousand Oaks, CA: Sage.

life, but in each case, the respondents explained that their awareness was often developed in response to their observations of differential treatment based on social differences.

One candidate of colour located herself in the status of *Ambivalence*. In terms of her self-definition and associations, this respondent indicated that she was ambivalent about her status with both Whites and Blacks. She explained in a follow-up interview, "I've had racism, I guess from both sides. You know, for some I'm not black enough; for others I'm too black." Noteworthy, as well, were two candidates of colour who placed themselves at "Status 3"– Immersion/Emersion Status—whereby own-group idealization and commitment are strong. Individuals located within this stage sometimes accentuate their ethno-racial identity by way of their dress, language codes and own-group formations.

Obstacles to RID growth

Participants perceived three main obstacles to achieving growth in their racial identity development: personal, programmatic and institutional. At the personal level, family commitments and part-time employment made it difficult for some to engage in extracurricular activities with other racialized groups. Such activities across cultural lines, and through personal interactions, might include attending cultural events, doing extensive reading, and generally developing an awareness of their own biases and privileges.

At the programmatic level, that is, the structure, content and pedagogical arrangements of the teacher education program itself, participants identified a number of obstacles to their growth. Some found the program structure was too tight and there were time restrictions on how issues should naturally evolve. Extended exploration, information processing, and critical reflection on the "difficult knowledge" of race were often curtailed. One participant of colour comments:

> We weren't ready for that [critical discussion on racial diversity]; emotions got stirred up, and there was no chance to debrief or talk through everything. You can't do it with 80 people in the class. I just felt that we should have [been] warned that this would stir up emotions. It is an excellent topic, but I am not pleased with the way it was handled. Some white people in the program have bonded even more to talk about how pissed off they were and created a bigger rift among certain people...

Such an observation was borne out by a white participant:

I have become more defensive being a white person in this program, which is very pro-minority, anti-racist,... like the white person was given the shaft in this program, discussed in stereotypical ways, and viewed as the reason for all of the oppression. Historically, it is true, but I got defensive as a white person in the program; that everything was anti-white. I felt that way; any anger that was expressed was directed at the white person.

While these perceptions of participants on both sides of the racial divide suggest program structure as an impediment to interrogating "race," it is clearly documented in the research literature that any critical engagement with this topic in the cross-race pedagogical domain, even if well managed, will likely evoke such emotions as guilt, anxiety, discomfort, defensiveness, denial, anger, or hostility (Fine et al. 1997; Helms 1995; Kailin 1989; Roman 1993; Tatum 1992). However, program structure must provide an environment where healthy tensions can foster individual growth and transformation.

The final obstacle to growth identified by some participants is that of practicum school (institutional) culture. Researchers' observations in classrooms and follow-up interviews with the participants revealed limited engagement with anti-racism pedagogy. In effect, the participants continued to reproduce celebratory multiculturalism rather than critically exploring with their students the systemic barriers to racial equity in school and community. Some perceived the practicum environment as one with the pre-set, standardized curriculum and remarked upon the rigid testing procedures taught by inflexible teachers who saw no room for what they described as the "soft curriculum" (Solomon and Allen 2001). The following comment represents the perceptions of a participant:

As a teacher candidate [pre-service teacher] I don't have any power to teach what I want in the classroom.

Others perceived the school culture as rather hierarchical, with rigid power relations (see Beach, 1999). In such structures there appear to be unwritten rules of engagement between school personnel and pre-service guests that lead to what Menter (1989) terms "teaching practice stasis"—an unwillingness to disrupt the status quo.

In the next section we discuss the implications of integrating racial identity issues into teacher education scholarship.

IMPLICATIONS FOR TEACHER EDUCATION

The study of racial identity development models in a pre-service teacher education program has suggested a number of implications for the preparation of professionals for work in racially diverse environments. The success of using such models depends on factors that evolved from the findings of this study: conceptual and theoretical framing of models; model application in diverse settings; selection of pre-service teachers and the provision of appropriate school cultures and learning environments.

Conceptual Framing of Racial Identity Development Models

Because of the complexities of identity formation, RID model use in pre-service teacher education must necessarily be selective. It should be used for raising consciousness—why individuals come to think and act in prescribed ways toward the "racial other." Use of the RID model should be growth-orientated, to help individuals chart their development progression to a more enlightened status for engaging in effective anti-racism work.

With this goal in mind, RID model users should be mindful of the pitfalls of model applications and be prepared to navigate around the problems unearthed in this study, and others reported in the research literature. Use of the model(s) could cause a problematic tendency to homogenize racial groups and to work with them as undifferentiated and stable. Also, educators might overlook the complex interplay of race and racism with other forms of marginalization, e.g., classism, sexism, or ethnocentrism.

Taking account of such limitations to RID model application, teacher educators should consider supplementing these models with other measures designed to raise consciousness about race and its impact in society, and to plan appropriate interventions. Such measures must move well beyond a primary focus on individuals, assessing knowledge, understanding and acceptance that are conceptually influenced by an uncritical multicultural perspective and a psychological model of change. A simplistic focus perpetuates the multicultural myth that more knowledge of diverse cultures will bring greater understanding and ultimately solve the problem of racial inequity in schooling.

Instruments used in consciousness-building exercises should also provide the means for pre-service teachers to interrogate the institutional and social context within which racial inequality operates. There must be discussion of power relations and racism's every-day operation at the school level, with a focus on critical thinking, to provide a more progressive and empowering education.

RID Model Application

A model's utility is highly dependent on the extent to which it can be transformed to suit individual and programmatic needs. Based on our experience in applying an RID model to pre-service teacher education, anyone using the RID model should ensure that both structure(s) and support(s) are in place in order to work with the following issues:

- The range and complexities of racial identities that may surface among participants and the need to adjust the working model to be more inclusive of variant groups;
- Participants' tendency to respond in emotionally debilitating ways that may pre-empt the transformative possibilities of the program. As Roman (1993) suggests, educators must seek out sound strategies to work with unproductive "white defensiveness" which may tend to polarize groups;
- The selection and development of practicum environments where pre-service teachers can implement their racial identity growth plans. Too often the institutional culture of practicum schools are perceived to be conservative, hierarchical in their power relations and preoccupied with externally-imposed academic standards and evaluation procedures. These conditions may limit teachers' professional growth in a racially diverse environment.

These are some of the challenges to which teacher educators must respond in order to integrate issues of race, racial identities, and anti-racism pedagogy in teacher education scholarship. No longer can a profession so central to the socialization of the next generation of citizens claim that "race doesn't matter" in a racialized world.

ENDNOTES

1. Although requested to self-identify in terms of heritage/ethnicity, a number of participants (mostly Whites) resisted hyphenization and chose to describe themselves only as "Canadian."
2. The 36 volunteers in the RID program were still fully integrated with their larger cohort of 80 plus for all course work.

chapter six

Cross-Race Dyad Partnerships in Pre-service Teacher Education

INTRODUCTION

The rhetoric of collaboration, cooperation and partnership has become increasingly popular in contemporary teacher education scholarship. Educational observers document the principle, practice, nature and political context of partnerships as educators engage in a variety of peer-centred professional developments variously labelled "peer coaching," "colleague consultation," "peer clinical supervision," and "peer assisted learning" (Boothe, Furlong, and Wilkins 1990; Glatthorn 1987; McFaul and Cooper 1984; Watters and Ginns 1997). But as schooling becomes more racially and culturally diverse, how may such a movement toward cooperative learning be realized, across racial and ethnocultural boundaries, in societies that tend toward own-group cleavage and racial homophily? How may teacher educators reverse this tendency and create an environment where teachers of different racial and ethnocultural backgrounds can engage collaboratively and collegially in a genuine, long-lasting appreciation of each other's norms, values, traditions and perspectives?

This study was based on the rationale that teachers' cross-race collaboration during the process of learning to teach would break down racial barriers, tackle sensitive racial and cultural issues and provide models of inter-group collaboration. Too often in the traditional practicum classroom, potentially contentious issues of social difference (race, ethnicity, social class, gender and sexuality) remain marginal to the curriculum, especially if such discourse challenges the conservative culture of schools. This study explores a new model for field-based teacher education that provides the structural arrangements for pre-service teacher partnerships to function productively in practicum classrooms.

To heighten the impact of diversity and difference, using the RID model in peer partnerships tests an approach in which teachers of dominant and minority racial backgrounds have extended opportunities to develop their teaching abilities and professional relationships in a collaborative and positive interdependent manner. We believe that the potential benefits of this format would be that racially and ethnoculturally diverse students would experience a curriculum and pedagogy infused with knowledge and perspective(s) beyond those of their associate teacher.[1]

THEORETICAL FRAMEWORK

The theoretical framework for this study evolved from two strands in the research literature. The first concept is that the practice of cooperative learning makes the essential linkages of this pedagogical approach between different levels of the schooling process and teacher education. The second is that inter-ethnic or interracial contact and collaboration introduces the issue of schooling in heterogeneous societies and provides a model for the development of a synergetic cross-group learning environment for pre-service teachers.

Cooperative Learning
We conceived of pairing pre-service teachers as a means of increasing cross-group exposure.

> As social beings that learn our language from each other, enhance our abilities to think through interactions with each other, and develop our voices by learning what is different about our perspectives from others, those other beings in our social communities become our greatest treasures. (Thayer-Bacon 1998, 209)

Thayer-Bacon's insights point to the necessity of utilizing other people as a resource for social development. Yet, theoretical and empirical works have documented the limited extent to which educational enterprises have embraced cooperation, positive interdependence and the use of co-workers or co-learners as resources. The empirical literature has reported the social and academic benefits of supportive peer culture of middle and high school students (Aljose and Joyner 1990; Beane 1990; Slavin 1983). But at the professional education level, and particularly in pre-service teacher education, the emerging research documents the need for a more collaborative approach to learning to teach (Hawkey 1994 and 1995; Norquay 1996; Su 1990 and 1992; Watson 1995).

In her large-scale study of the professional socialization of pre-service teachers in the United States, Su (1992) found that in their practicum experience, candidates had limited opportunities for collegial interactions. "[They] confront a 'sink-or-swim' situation in physical isolation. The way most beginners are inducted into teaching therefore leaves them doubly alone" (249). She identifies a number of factors that may have inhibited the development of a collaborative peer culture: large group programs that impede cooperative, interactive relationships; the short duration of some teacher education programs that leave little time for relationships to develop; and the absence of after-class socialization activities resulting from family and job obligations (1990, 381). Su challenges the individualism and the mechanistic technification of learning to teach, and advocates instead a reformulated peer culture that expands candidates' moral and intellectual horizons.

Cooperative learning outweighs the benefits of conservative teacher education. Watson (1995) claims candidates who have the opportunity to work within cooperative learning environments demonstrate greater material retention over time, learn at higher cognitive levels, feel positively about themselves and the subject matter, and become more skilled in interpersonal interactions (210). In the context of race and ethnocultural diversity, Watson emphasizes building collaborative environments for cultural understanding. She suggests, "cooperative learning is effective in prejudice reduction ... and in meeting the academic and social needs of at risk students" (213).

Hawkey's (1994 and 1995) and Norquay's (1996) research on school-based teacher education is most informative in developing alternative paradigms based on peer support in the classroom. Starting from the premise that peers are an underused resource, Hawkey examines ways in which structured peer support operates within the reflective practitioner model of learning to teach. More specifically, her research focuses on the nature of peer post-lesson interaction and the extent to which novices contribute to the professional development of their peers.

Beyond the giving of basic support, probing questions emerge from more interactive conversations, as the reflective practitioner model would dictate. These interactions, Hawkey (1994) suggests, "demonstrate a readiness to air (such) concerns with a peer. It may be that within the familiar non-threatening environment of working with another peer, novices are more willing to express anxieties than with a tutor or mentor" (142). While Hawkey concludes that there are benefits in collaborative planning, teaching and post-lesson conferences, she suggests the need for further research to determine the extent to which peers can appropriately challenge as well as offer support to one another. Both activities are essential to the development of critical pedagogical reflection. Other key questions emerging from Hawkey's (1995, 182) research that are addressed by this study are:

- What and how do peers learn from each other?
- What is the effect of the prevailing school culture on collaborative learning to teach?
- What is the effect of different factors (such as previous experience and outlook, gender style, and stage in development) on the dynamics of peers working together?

A key factor for exploration in this study is race. How are issues of race, race relations and anti-racism taken up in teacher education scholarship? How are pre-service teachers prepared to work in multiracial schools, and how do participants in teacher education respond to an anti-racism pedagogy? The introduction of the "race factor" in cooperative learning environments may well generate a kind of synergy that is more complex to unravel.

Cross-Race Collaboration in Learning to Teach

The persistence of "ethnic encapsulation" and racial homophily throughout elementary and secondary schooling (Hallinan and Teixeria 1987; Solomon 1992; Tatum 1997) has led sociologists to believe that such patterns of social relations will likely persist in post-secondary institutions and professional schools. A disturbing trend in these studies is that, although there were opportunities for positive inter-group relationships, the gradual development of racial identities and same-group peer relations seem to polarize rather than build bridges between racial and ethnic groups.

Such a trend carries the potential to generate and perpetuate prejudice and stereotypes because of own-group cleavages and mutual ignorance. Group attitudes and perspectives make it difficult for them to learn from the norms, values, traditions, knowledge, competencies and experiences of the "other." The traditional teacher education curriculum and pedagogy do not interrogate candidates' worldviews, nor urge them to engage in critical self-reflection on their identities and their impact on learning to teach. Those teacher educators who attempt this process are met with covert and overt resistance (Ahlquist 1992; Sleeter 1992a). Indeed, the creation of a learning environment where candidates of diverse backgrounds can enrich each other's personal and professional lives and increase their teaching repertoires is never realized.

Teaching for Equity and Diversity

The design of the cross-race dyad system in this study transcends Sears' (1991) conception, and uses as its framework Lynch's (1987) inter-ethnic and interracial contact model to reduce inter-group polarization and entrenchment and build instead productive collaboration among student groups. Lynch proposes a change model that modifies not only individual (or group) characteristics, but also the structural and organizational characteristics of the learning environment. The main features of such an inter-ethnic and interracial contact model, adapted and summarized from Lynch (121) are:

- The contact must be equal status, and must be manifestly supported by the authority of the institution;
- The contact within the group should be on a collaborative basis, and there should be a similarity of competence level among the group members;
- The contacts should be continuous rather than transitory, and there should be opportunities to interact with outgroup members as individuals; and
- There should be explicit superordinate goals for the group as a whole, and the work of the group must stand a good chance of success.

The research literature has debated the merits and demerits of "contrived collegiality" in teacher professional development. On the demerit side of the ledger, Hargreaves (1991) found contrived collegiality to be an imposition (from school administrators), inflexible, inefficient, over-managed and one which overrides teacher professionalism. He concludes, "[It] is constitutive of socio-political and administrative systems that are less than fully serious about their rhetorical commitment to teacher empowerment" (69).

To the contrary, the contrived collegiality model utilized in this study of pre-service teachers emerges from what Hargreaves and others describe as the collaborative culture domain. Here, relationships are not prefigured but are shaped by such factors as classroom context, associate teachers' support, personality of dyad partners, their work rhythms and teaching experience. There is also an explicit understanding that partners who are incompatible will be given the opportunity to work individually, while productive and supportive relationships may continue beyond the predetermined termination time. Essentially, this model provides the structural arrangements for candidates to grow friendships across racial boundaries.

DESIGNING CROSS-RACE DYAD PARTNERSHIPS

Participants in the cross-race dyad system were candidates who were already admitted to York University's one-year Bachelor of Education program and who volunteered for the Urban Diversity Teacher Education.

From 1994 to1997, three cohorts each of 44 teacher candidates were selected, representing the racial and ethnocultural diversity of the school communities served by the university. The design of the program dictated the selection of two evenly matched racial groups: firstly, candidates of European-Canadian heritage, often referred to as "White" or as the dominant group—for example, those descended from British, Italian, Jewish, or French forebears—and secondly, racial minority candidates primarily of African- and Asian-Canadian heritages—for example, those of first generation, as descendants of West Indian, Pakistani, Chinese and Japanese forebears.

At the outset, group-building activities at the university site provided the opportunity for participants to develop a strong cohort culture. Theory-based assignments emphasized collaboration, team planning and execution. Field placements in practicum schools were arranged in smaller cohorts of four, six or eight evenly proportioned Whites and candidates of colour. Cross-race partnerships of two participants per classroom evolved on the basis of their grade level choices; the essential directive being that those from the same racial group could not share the same classroom. These partnerships extended into the ethno-cultural communities served by the school, where teacher candidates were expected to engage in some form of social or educational project.

Program expectations were that dyad partners develop a working relationship, utilize each other's cultural knowledge, experiences and resources, jointly observe and discuss the teaching-learning process in their practicum classroom, jointly prepare and team-teach lessons, and participate as a team in post-lesson debriefings with their associate teacher. The associate teachers were veteran professionals selected by the school principals to host and mentor candidates placed in their classrooms. Orientation to the rationale and functioning of the dyad system was provided for all field-based personnel related to the program.

The dyad structure remained in effect for most of the candidates' practicum experience—two days per week throughout the year in addition to two teaching blocks of two weeks for the first and second terms. At the beginning of the second term, when candidates switched from the primary to junior division (or vice versa), they teamed with another partner who was again racially different. For the final teaching block of three weeks, three candidates had the option of working independent of a partner.

For the research component of the project, data gathering strategies included individual and focus-group interviews conducted by research assistants from White and People of Colour groups, the observation of dyad partners in their practicum settings, analysis of journal entries, and end-of-year written evaluations of the dyad system by all three cohorts (C1, C2, C3). Participants' selection for interviews was based on practicum personnel's (associate teachers, adjunct professors and practicum supervisors) perception of partnerships as achieving or not achieving the dyad system's objectives.

Over the three-year research period, approximately half of the 132 candidates participated in either individual or focus-group interviews. Interviews were semi-structured and explored such issues as previous exposure to extended across-race interaction; impact of the 'race factor' on learning to teach; specific opportunities to learn from the dyad partner about racially diverse classrooms; dyadic relationships as collaborative or competitive; equitable or inequitable treatment of partners by supervisory personnel; and the modelling of cross-race collaboration in the classroom. These were also key issues in the observation guide used in practicum classrooms and highlighted in participants' journal entries and end-of-year reflections.

For the analysis of these data the principles of "constant comparative" methods were employed (Glaser and Strauss 1967; Strauss 1987). Patterns and themes from the coded data of year one generated the questions for interrogation in subsequent years of the study. Triangulation of data from the different sources continued to strengthen perception of emerging patterns and helped formulate generalizations about dyad partnerships.

This qualitative approach was instrumental in capturing the feelings and experiences of teachers learning to teach collegially in a competitive school environment. The findings that follow are reported primarily through participants' narratives (pseudonyms used throughout) as they shared their positive experiences in the first part of this chapter, and in the second part, the challenges posed by social difference and racial preference in teacher education and teaching.

BENEFITS OF CROSS-RACE DYAD PARTNERSHIPS

The findings indicate that peer partnerships inject quality interaction into the process of learning to teach. Participant narratives revealed rich benefits in the development of pedagogical competencies and the provision of emotional support for partners. In the area of lesson preparation, dyad partners created opportunities to plan lessons at their practicum schools, at the teacher education site, on the telephone, and by visiting each other's homes. At the lesson presentation stage, dyad partners were equally enthusiastic about team-teaching and were anxious to learn from each other's teaching style, perspectives and experiences. The other dimension of learning to teach that was valued by dyad partners was post-lesson discussion. Often, these discussions between partners continued well beyond the associate teacher's contribution.

Researcher observation of these candidates in practicum classrooms and follow-up interviews with them revealed that candidates brought different strengths and weaknesses to their pedagogical tasks and gained from each other's experiences and teaching styles. At the emotional level, participants revealed the benefits of a peer support system to cope with the pressures of program intensity, the frustrations of a "lesson gone wrong," and the anxieties of learning to teach in competitive school cultures.

Of great note for this study are the benefits that were derived from participants' collaboration across racial borders. As will be detailed later, cross-race dyad partnerships provided the structure for candidates of different racial, ethnic and cultural heritages to develop productive work relationships, and to deal with diversity and difference in a positive and direct manner. Such partnerships helped to break down racial barriers, tackle sensitive racial and cultural issues, and explore divergent political perspectives and ideologies. Most importantly, cross-race partnerships prepared candidates to work competently with students and parents of racially diverse backgrounds. Beyond personal and professional growth, some revealed that lasting friendships resulted from these partnerships; relationships that extended beyond the classroom to their social lives.

It is important to clarify that the benefits of dyad partnerships are not always clearly articulated in candidates' narratives. They are often interwoven with the challenges encountered while exploring the sensitive issues of racial difference and diversity within the restricted time frame of an intensive nine-month teacher education program. The themes that follow capture the many ways candidates experienced the dyad system and its impact on their personal and professional growth.

Bridging Racial Barriers Through Sustained Dialogue

For both dominant and minority groups, the program structure and process traversed, to some extent, the "racial divide" that appeared insurmountable in their prior experiences in other institutional settings. The dyad system provided the organizational structure for inter-group collaboration in teacher education praxis. In keeping with Lynch's (1987) interethnic contact model, this structure moved well beyond the transitory, fleeting contacts often utilized by traditional programs to build understanding and working relationships across racial lines.[2] Such sustained contact provided candidates with the opportunity to explore, in a structured and supportive learning environment, race-based political ideologies, cultural norms, traditions and perceived "peculiarities."

The following is an example of such a collaboration:

> It was a good experience. We spent many hours talking about different things. He was wearing a Malcolm X t-shirt and I wondered to what extent he was sympathetic to black Muslims because if I had a public enemy number one it would be [that group]. So we talked about that. He was kind of curious about Judaism and we had a really good talk about that when we were doing our narrative assignment. It was supposed to take half an hour, but we just sat and chewed the fat. We talked about meaty issues like Black Power. We did have good conversations, but given the intensity of the program, its relatively short duration, the fact that there was little real time to get really acquainted without the pressure scenario, we didn't get to know each other as much as we might have. (C1:4, White Candidate)[3]

Dan Yon (2000) argues for the creation of discursive space within institutional structures for students to deal with their racial identities. The above excerpt from a teacher candidate's narrative provides insight into the partners limited previous exposure to and interaction with the "other," although they live in a society that embraces diversity in principle. Historically, racial groups in Canada as well as other Western societies such as the United States have lived parallel but not integrated social lives.

For candidates in this study, the potential benefits of being provided with discursive space to explore their respective "racial" identities were enormous. It increased their capacity for multiple perspectives and allowed them to reconstitute themselves as more open-minded and less ethnocentric individuals. Being provided, in the classroom, with alternative discursive experiences prepare teachers to create an environment for constructive dialogue. Such teachers can foster sustained dialogue across the "racial divide", which we hope will help to develop children's capacity to embrace diversity and difference in the classroom and beyond.

The Acquisition of Awareness and Competence to Function in Cross-Race Domains

Participants emerging from racially homogeneous communities and schools came to teacher education with limited knowledge and often a stereotypic preconception of "the other." Through cross-race partnership, the candidates were introduced to an insider's perspectives on other cultural terrains. They provided entry points to each other's ethnocultural communities. The teacher education program's extended practicum required candidates to know more intimately the communities served by the school. Here, the dyad partnerships provided candidates with a guided immersion into the complex life and functioning of ethno-racial communities and the school's role within them.

Such guided intervention also provided awareness of the cultural knowledge, traditions and artifacts that are potentially school curriculum materials. The excerpt that follows explains how such exposure helps to develop the self-confidence and competence to interact professionally across racial boundaries in school settings:

> Being in a dyad [partnership] gave some direction, it gave some focus, and the focus was two people from diverse backgrounds, and in this case specifically, two different races. Prior to working with my partner I don't think I was prepared as I am right now. What I've learned this year in the lecture room, in my own course work, and my practicum classroom was that I wasn't prepared before to work closely with someone from a different background. This experience was certainly one of the strong points about this program. (C2:11, Candidate of Colour)

Because Whites' lived experiences were almost exclusively in dominant group institutions, their prior level of functioning was not contingent upon familiarity with or knowledge about the "racial other." And as Robertson-Baghel's (1998) research shows, the later in life that inter-group contact occurs, the more difficult it becomes to shed negative stereotypes and assumptions about the "racial other."

Positive Social Outcomes of Cross-Race Partnerships

Journal entries, the observation of dyad partners at the teacher education site and in the practicum settings and interviews with the partners indicated that cross-race social relationships developed to various degrees from these structures. Post-program follow-up studies showed that the strong emotional bonds that developed moved well beyond the classroom and into the social lives of partners during and after their initial teacher education. Two years after graduation, cohorts were still meeting regularly as an informal group to socialize and talk about their work and other ventures. Such reunions were also a source of support for those challenged by the conservatism and inequities of the school cultures in which they taught, and a clearing house of information for those who were still seeking employment or exploring further professional and academic studies. The excerpt that follows indicates the quality of the reciprocal relationship across racial lines:

> We could be very comfortable about things. What I wanted to learn and what I was curious about I could ask her [dyad partner] openly and we dealt with things from there. We had lot of laughs from things that we thought about each other. She would even say that up until now she had never had a really close white friend. As for myself, I only had one close friend who is Black and one close friend who is Asian. Other than that my friends are mostly Whites. But my partner is more like a best friend. (C3:15, White Candidate)

In Sleeter's (1993) work on the structuring of immersion experiences of the white candidates she reinforces the importance of an approach that develops "some emotional bonding with members of the [racial minority] group, [which] can propel serious re-examination of his or her perspective" (169). The dyad arrangement satisfied the needs of Whites expressed by Sleeter and created the opportunity for both groups to engage in sustained social relationships.

Probably the most important experience of white candidates in cross-race partnerships was learning how racism operates in institutions such as schools. As one candidate of colour discovers, "It is necessary that you pair a person of colour with one of the dominant group because it's putting the whole issue of race, racism and power relations 'in your face.'"

Dominant group individuals in Canadian society have habitually denied the existence of racism in their institutions (Alladin 1996; Henry et al. 1995; Solomon and Levine-Rasky 1994). Until this stage in their education, some white participants had maintained that the educational system is meritocractic, and teachers within fair, impartial and "colour-blind" (Robertson-Baghel 1998; Solomon 1995b). This naive or ideologically strategic stance is partly responsible for widespread resistance to anti-racism pedagogy developed to eliminate racism in schools and society (Carr and Klassen 1997; Dei 1996a; James 1995a; Solomon and Levine-Rasky 1996a, 1996b). People of colour who reported racist victimization were often perceived to be "crying wolf." Without a perceptive and impartial third party witness to the perpetration of racism, this subordinating and demoralizing act had become a "witnessless" crime.

Dyad partnerships provided Whites with the opportunity to witness how school agents routinely and often unconsciously engage in differential behaviour based on race. They were now privy to the process of racial marginalization, explored in the next section, as they watched their partners of colour denied privileges, assumed to be less capable than Whites, and over-scrutinized as they learned to teach. As insightful pre-service teachers, they concluded that such differential school practices were also afforded to students of colour. Given such an exposure to and acknowledgement of the stark realities of racism in school, the dyad system will be better able to prepare white teachers to respond to individual and institutional racism.[4]

How did participants of colour benefit from cross-race dyad partnerships? Because some have had to operate almost exclusively in dominant group institutions with white colleagues, critics argue that their learning curve in the dyad system might not have been as steep as that of their white partners. But it is not difficult to see how colleagues of colour who are immigrants from societies where they were the majority might gain valuable insights into the "cultural capital" required to penetrate the "culture of power" in dominant group institutions. By their close association with their white colleagues they developed a better understanding of power relations in institutional settings, and learned the skills required to negotiate such power and concomitant resources. Delpit's (1988) pedagogical strategy of exposing minority children to the culture of power is applicable here for these candidates of colour. Their white partner's explanation of how this operates was of benefit to candidates of colour.

For some, their "equity-conscious" white partners provided a "reality check" on their attitudes toward the dominant group. Here, one elaborates:

> Interacting with a lot of dominant group candidates in my [teacher education] class I became very discouraged. They were not naming their power and privilege, and when you call them on it, they reacted negatively. I started to get very discouraged and I kept generalizing, "Oh my, they [white people] are all like that; they'll never understand." But my dyad partner, she is my reality check. By her behaviour and understanding, she was the person who said, "No, all the people from the dominant group are not like that." (C3:17, Candidate of Colour)

Dyad partnerships temporarily sheltered candidates of colour from overt forms of racism. Although this study uncovered evidence of "latent" racism, equity conscious white partners acted as a deterrent to overt practices of racism by school personnel. As we shall see later in this study, perceptive Whites have often detected racism directed at their partners and some have strategized to act against it. Such a response had the potential to make the practicum environment a more wholesome and equitable place for pre-service teachers of colour.

To conclude, the findings of this section indicate that the organizational characteristics of learning environments can be transformed to create opportunities for the acquisition of cross-group awareness and competence to work effectively with social difference. The awareness of how environments may be transformed to facilitate "cross-border" learning is an essential awakening for those preparing to teach in racially diverse settings.

CHALLENGES TO DYAD PARTNERSHIPS

Despite the many benefits of cross-race collaboration in teaching, this study uncovered personal, institutional and systemic factors that challenged the concepts and practices of the dyad partnerships. Extremely damning for multiracial school systems are the ways that these factors interact with race to restrict, marginalize and subordinate candidates of colour in their quest to become teachers.

Perhaps the biggest challenge to partnerships is differential treatment of candidates based on race. The findings strongly implicate some practicum personnel (associate teachers and adjunct professors), in perceiving and responding to candidates of colour as subordinate and deficient members in the dyad partnership. Such a perception had tremendous influence on the communication process between dyad members and practicum supervisors, on candidate-driven curriculum innovations, and on the level of control and authority minority candidates were allowed to exercise in practicum classrooms. The following narratives from both dominant and racial minorities make explicit the debilitating and dysfunctional impact of racism, not only on candidates of colour, but also on their dominant group partners.

Anxiety-Generating Scrutiny of Candidates of Colour
Practicum supervisors' microscopic examination of candidates of colour as objects in the classroom proved to be anxiety provoking, tension-ridden, destabilizing and a serious impediment to learning to teach. A white candidate describes this tension:

The AP [Adjunct Professor] was brutal. I would have been paranoid if I'd undergone the scrutiny [my dyad partner received]. I wondered if it was because he was a male or because he was from a very different culture from those who were evaluating him. We had probably about one third of the classroom who were Muslim so the students were very fond of him and identified with him very closely. It was frustrating being his partner because it was impossible to teach with the level of anxiety that there was on both of us. (C1:1, White Candidate)

The anxiety-generating scrutiny experienced by candidates of colour in the practicum setting extended to their curriculum content and pedagogy. In their attempts to introduce issues of multiculturalism and anti-racism pedagogy into traditional classrooms they experienced discomfort, feelings of incompetence and censorship of their teaching materials and choice of curricula materials. Such seeds of self-doubt planted by supervisors have the potential to restrict and stifle creativity, innovation, and critical agency in practicum classrooms.

Although equity and social justice have been introduced into progressive teacher education scholarship, discontinuities plague the passage of such issues from university lecture-rooms to practicum classrooms. Resistance to the inclusion of critical multiculturalism, anti-racism and other equity issues into the curriculum of schools whose culture is White and mainstream is well documented in the Canadian (Carr and Klassen 1997; Solomon and Levine-Rasky 1996a and b), British (Gillborn 1995; Troyna and Williams 1986), and American (Delpit 1995; King 1991; Sleeter 1992b) research literature. Faced with such inhospitable learning environments participants of colour not only had their self-confidence trampled upon and ideals compromised, but they ended up conforming to rather conservative notions of curriculum just to get through their program of teacher education.

Interpretation of Difference as Deficit

The findings of this study clearly show that the candidates of colour, when compared with their white colleagues, were perceived as deficient or incapable. Such perceptions of the associate teachers resulted in poor evaluations and restricted opportunities for candidates of colour:

First term was awful because of the perceptions that our associate teacher had of him [dyad partner of colour]. I spent a great deal of time defending him and trying to get her [associate teacher] to see that his methods were just different, they weren't worse, they were just different. I was better at mimicking what was expected of us... I thought that was very, very unfair. (C1:2, White Candidate)

This quotation raises a number of issues in teacher education. The first has to do with methodological essentialism and the expectation that candidates learn to teach by imitating veteran teachers. This approach potentially reproduces methodological homogeneity in an environment where the student population is becoming more diverse, and requires pedagogically responsive and contextually flexible teaching. Another issue for candidates is that the apprenticeship model of learning to teach quickly sorts and labels those who mimic as good learners and others who don't as deficient. Such value judgements encourage prospective teachers to fit into the hidden curriculum of associate teachers and discourage them from engaging in critical pedagogy.

Finally, the perception of candidates of colour as deficient restricted their teaching opportunities in practicum classrooms, as the following excerpt indicates:

The associate teacher was still at the stage where she was trying to give the basic steps to my dyad partner. But when I went on my own I was to do more open activities and "risk take". Without my dyad partner I was able to have control of the room, where prior to this, the associate teacher did not feel secure leaving the room with my dyad partner there. (C2:13, White Candidate)

The cross-race dyad system reawakened the notion that people of colour need Whites as a crutch to survive in dominant group institutions. Despite the clarified objectives of paired sharing across the racial divide, some associate teachers remained entrenched in their ideology that candidates of colour will be a burden to their white counterparts and the teaching profession.

Marginalization in the Communication Process

Race also mediated the pattern of communication between associate teachers and dyad partners. Researchers' observations within practicum classrooms revealed that the quality and frequency of associate teachers' interaction with white candidates far outweighed those with candidates of colour. Such preference is evident in the following interview excerpt:

I find that most of the time when Phyllis [partner of colour] and I deal with authorities, people are usually paying more attention to me... . I think people look at me more; they make more eye contact and give me more feedback. I mean, they talk to Phyllis with the occasional reference, even if I don't say anything, so I find that discriminating. Our first associate teacher was very much like that; he gave a lot more attention to me. I pointed that out to Phyllis and she kind of brushed it off; but I think it would bother me. I didn't do anything about it. If I had done something about it I think it would have been like the white girl is saving the day. So, I let Phyllis handle it the way she wanted to. (C1:6, White Candidate)

In a practicum environment where ongoing verbal communication is an essential dimension of learning to teach, the marginalized are obviously disadvantaged, especially in a competitive school culture. These cross-race communication patterns are laden with meanings and send strong messages about the hierarchies that exist in the social structure of the classroom and in the larger social system. The meanings white candidates attached to their communication experience point to broken bridges across the racial divide in North American societies; there seems to be a lack of connectedness between dominant and minority racial groups, and an apparent discomfort in some cross-race interactions. While the dyad structure provided an opportunity for growth in cross-race relationships, developing strategies to change the racial culture at the institutional level is a great challenge.[5]

Competitive Individualism

The teacher candidates' partnership was structured to be a collaborative exercise:

I think it [dyad system] was established to allow children to see people working together, not just the same people, but people from different ethnic groups working together collaboratively. I think it was also created to model for the children mutual cooperation and respect. (D1-2:3)

The dyad situation is not supposed to be a competitive thing. It's something where you're supposed to be working together; it's not a competition. I find it getting like a competitive thing where I have to outdo this person and I have to prove something. (D1-2:7)

The quotes above reflect candidates' general knowledge of the program objectives explicitly stated or implied. Despite such an understanding, some teacher candidates' competitive and individualistic behaviours often derailed attempts to nurture cooperation among dyads and rendered them dysfunctional. One dimension of competition is that driven by personality or socialization, or both. But at the broader level, institutional regularities and social relations within school foster active competition between dyad partners, and by not establishing ground rules for collaboration, school personnel inadvertently foster competition. Troyna and Williams (1986, 107) argue that the education system is based on "competitive individualism geared to producing an achievement hierarchy ..." controlled increasingly by government. Such a powerful combination of factors against collaboration makes it a major challenge for teacher educators to implement a pedagogy that reduces the competitive culture within schools.

IMPLICATIONS FOR TEACHER EDUCATION

The study was designed to examine the extent to which inter-group collaboration advances teacher education and teaching. The findings, however, provide deeper insights into the personal and institutional construction of race and racism. How must we theorize about this racism? Sleeter (1993) and Wellman (1993) urge us to examine structural arrangements among racial groups in the larger society, since schools are inextricably related to the social order.

This debilitating social problem is not unique to Canada; research conducted elsewhere (e.g., the United Kingdom and the U.S.) provide similar findings of schooling in these social contexts. This structural analysis of schooling points to the protection of power and privilege by those in a position to defend it. Some white teachers in this study perceive teaching as a race privilege profession and protect it from "the other" in the most inequitable ways. They suspend their moral accountability in constructing candidates of colour as deficient, incompetent and as "a white man's burden."

Teacher educators must therefore accept the challenge of confronting racism and working proactively with candidates and their associate teachers to minimize its impact. According to Short (1992) there is no effective mechanism to screen racist prospective teachers from the profession, and no foolproof approach to detect racist practitioners in schools. In addition, it might be futile to try to eradicate deep-seated, ideologically entrenched racism, to change those with the pathological need to subordinate others, or to engage those who are unresponsive to rational discourse (Allport 1954; Short 1992). Instead, teacher educators must focus on those pre-service and in-service teachers who engage in "unintentional racism" (Department of Education and Science 1985), or "dysconscious racism," an uncritical habit of accepting and internalizing dominant group justifications for racial inequalities in schools and society (King 1991).

In summary, the findings indicate that the program structure provided a discursive space that drew candidates out of their own-group cleavages and into a broader inter-group domain. Sustained dialogue, an ongoing professional and social interaction between partners, and exposure to the racial nuances of their practicum schools enabled them to evolve from a superficial understanding of racial difference and race privilege to a more critical perspective of how race impacts people's lives in institutional settings. These critical insights prepared prospective teachers, especially Whites, to move away from their liberal "colour-blind" view of working with racial diversity, and to occupy a more critical "colour-conscious" perspective. Such a heightened sensitivity to race and schooling is essential for working equitably in today's multiracial schools.

Further, cross-race dyad partnerships provided strategic entry points into other's race and ethnocultural domains. This dyadic approach to community fieldwork provided candidates with insiders' perspectives into the lived experiences of the "other." This awareness allowed candidates to make informed and worthwhile social, cultural and educational contributions to the children and youth of these communities. By the same token, candidates became aware of the rich cultural resources that could potentially enhance the school curriculum.

For the teacher educator, this research reinforces the fact that environments can be restructured to achieve desired outcomes. Throughout the study, candidates acknowledged that this restructuring of relationships "generated excitement," "served as an eye-opener," and "provided for confrontation with racism and power relations." This research signals the urgent need for teacher educators to abandon their conventional approaches and explore transformative arrangements that are more in tune with a rapidly evolving multiracial society.

But there are challenges to overcome in the implementation of progressive designs such as cross-race dyad partnerships. Lynch's (1987) inter-ethnic and interracial contact model stipulates that for contact arrangements to be productive, they must be manifestly supported by the authority structure in which they function. This study uncovered the ways in which practicum school agents subverted the dyad system and restricted its potential. They did not perceive and treat Whites and Candidates of Colour as equals; in fact, some engaged in the production of incompetence in some Candidates of Colour. Further, within the competitive culture of practicum schools, the principle of collaboration gave way to competitive individualism.

These findings have serious implications for teacher education in multiracial societies. Teacher educators are challenged to develop and implement an approach to inter-group collaboration that is less vulnerable to the institutional culture of racism. Field-based practica, as a vital dimension of learning to teach, must operate within an "equity conscious" environment. Teacher educators must work toward the development of a more controlled pre-service environment that ensures continuity of equity principles from the university lecture-room to practicum classrooms. Practicum personnel must therefore embrace the principles and practices of equity, social justice and anti-racism education. This is an issue we will revisit later in this text.

ENDNOTES

1. In this study, teacher candidates are those who are engaged in initial teacher education. They are also referred to as "student teachers" or "pre-service teachers." Associate teachers are those teachers in whose classrooms teacher candidates are placed for field-based practica. They are also referred to as "host teachers," "cooperating teachers," or "mentor teachers." In some teacher education models, associate teachers are seen as "master teachers" to whom candidates are apprenticed. The Adjunct Professor is the liaison between practicum schools and the teacher education facility and has the responsibility of evaluating candidates. The Practicum Supervisor is university-based and is ultimately responsible for the practicum component of teacher education.

2. Some teacher education programs encourage visits to ethnic communities and interviews with racial or ethnic minorities to develop familiarity with difference and diversity. In such situations contacts are superficial and transitory, and the interviewer-interviewee relationship is unequal. This is typical of the traditional anthropological research approach to "studying the natives."

3. Interview respondents are identified by codes: C1:4, White Candidate, indicates, Cohort year one, respondent 4, who is a white teacher candidate.

4. There is no guarantee that white candidates will intervene on their partner's behalf since some of them benefit from this inequitable treatment by school personnel. This is what some observers describe as "living off the avails of racism."

5. At the classroom and school levels, white candidates have started engaging in a strategy of moving their partners of colour from the margins to the inner circle of communication through the process of deflection. This strategy using verbal and non-verbal cues entails deflecting questions and comments from school personnel to their dyad partners. Inclusive communicative relationships develop in a non-confrontational way.

chapter seven

Community Involvement:
A Service Learning Approach
to Teacher Education

INTRODUCTION

Over the years, educational institutions have forged various linkages with the communities in which they are located. Working on the premise that schools and communities must build positive work relationships for the good of children, new forms of interactions, collaborations and partnerships have evolved. Formal as well as informal structures have been put in place to facilitate such partnerships. For example, the informal parent-teacher associations of the past have given way to the more formal, state-mandated school councils in many educational jurisdictions. Current school reforms also support the formal involvement of secondary students in the life of the community. They engage in workplace and career familiarization projects, gaining valuable work experience in business, industry and social sectors. There has also been an unprecedented incursion of business into the curriculum and life of the school.[1]

In-service teachers have forged a somewhat tenuous relationship with communities served by their schools. They often "invite" selected community groups into the school on special occasions and for particular activities. But the extent to which teachers get involved in the social, cultural and political life of the community is debatable. Teachers' roles as members of a dominant group, middle class professionals, often separate them from the urban, working-class, inner city, culturally diverse communities in which they work. As these communities evolve, educators' interactions with them become more complex and challenging. They teach in heterogeneous communities for which they had little or no formal preparation. Despite the evolving diversity of most western societies, teacher education institutions continue to prepare teachers for homogeneous communities that are fast disappearing.

The need for pre-service teachers to engage meaningfully with communities while learning to teach cannot be overemphasized. Teacher educators must build into their pedagogy the theoretical framework and the formal structures for candidates to gain the awareness, knowledge and competencies to work effectively with and in communities. John Dewey, educational philosopher and practitioner, engendered a progressive educational movement that is built on the principle and practice of active and constructive participation in community life (Dewey 1900).

In this chapter we provide the theoretical context of teachers' experiential learning in their communities of practice and synthesize the salient principles that guide such practice. These principles guided the design of a community involvement and service-learning model that was implemented in a pre-service program. The learning experiences of participants are well documented in their own critical reflection on their community action. The chapter concludes with some of the challenges and possibilities of community learning and its implications for teacher education.

THEORETICAL UNDERPINNINGS

The concept of extending structured learning from classrooms to the communities they serve emerges from initiatives designed to link institutional and community learning at all levels of schooling. These initiatives are variously labelled in the research literature as "service learning" (Hones 1997; Kahne and Westheimer 1996; O'Grady 2000; Rhoads and Howard 1998); "community field experience" (Zeichner and Melnick 1996); "community-referenced learning" (Kluth 2000), "community experiential learning" (Boyle-Baise and Efiom 2000); "situated social practice or situated learning" (Lave 1991).[2] Yet others characterize this form of pedagogy as "an encounter with strangers;" "an encounter with otherness;" and "dialogue across difference" (Radest 1993). Such a range of labels reflects the ways educators conceptualize and implement schooling intervention into the life of communities.

Boyle-Baise and Efiom (2000) conceptualize service learning as "a process of experiential, relational learning: Students learn from the community, from personal experiences, and from classmates" (212).

Using John Dewey's notion of education as experiential Hones (1997) sums up what he thinks service learning ought to accomplish:

service learning allows for an educational process that is problem-posing, wherein students can identify, investigate, and attempt to solve problems that affect the lives of other members of society. Through engaging with others of different ethnicities, social classes, and language backgrounds, students can learn from and become invested in a larger community that stretches the limits of their experience, their imagination and their sense of self. (4)

Implicit in the Hones quote above and the broader literature on service learning is a model that links critical thinking about education and schooling, civic responsibility and community action. Kluth (2000) makes an important linkage here between "community-referenced learning" and postmodernism that urges teachers to be unwavering in questioning "what they know and how they know it" (21). She continues:

Postmodernism asks teachers to consider the power structures, implicit and explicit curricular, and values in the classroom.... . When students function as investigators and actors in the community, they are generating knowledge for themselves and constructing their own meanings of their learning. Postmodernism supports this type of investigation, active learning, and questioning of current knowledge. (21)

The research literature suggests an academic service learning model that links critical thinking about education, civic responsibility and community action. The notion of civic responsibility of educators to view education as a democratic project that fosters social justice and social equity is well documented in the literature (Carr and Hartnett 1996; Koli 2000; Portelli 1996). Such a model provides a social analysis of education that challenges the way schools work with such issues as social difference (for example, race, ethnicity, gender, sexual orientation, social class, disabilities), power relations and power hierarchies in institutional settings and society at large (Hones 1997; Green 1996; Ladson-Billings 1995).

Howard (1998) describes this synergistic model of academic service learning as integrated and reciprocally related in the teaching learning process—each experience (in the university setting, the practicum school and the community) informing and transforming the other. (See Figure 17.1.)

The notion that service learning must also be political was the central theme in Kahne and Westheimer's (1996) work *In the service of what? The politics of service learning*. Here they provide a conceptual framework for understanding service learning curricula that are operating in the moral, political and intellectual domains, and offer distinctions between the goals of charity and those of change.

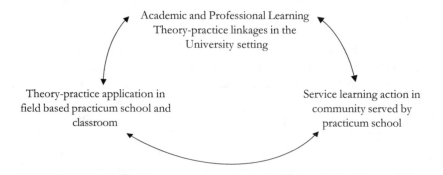

Figure 7.1
A Synergistic Model of Teacher Education

Academic and Professional Learning
Theory-practice linkages in the
University setting

Theory-practice application in
field based practicum school and
classroom

Service learning action in
community served by
practicum school

According to Kahne and Westheimer, educators who perceive service learning as charity develop a curriculum that emphasizes giving, and see the service of clients as falling in the moral domain. Experience-based learning opportunities, critical thinking in contextually varied environments, and the promotion of interdisciplinarity all fall in the intellectual domain; whereas the value of altruism, volunteerism and civic responsibility fall in the political domain.

Conversely, when the emphasis of service learning is on change, and transformation moral goals are on caring, intellectual goals favour transformative experiences, and political goals are social reconstructionism. Kahne and Westheimer argue that the politics of service learning must look beyond the rhetoric of altruism to interrogate the structural injustices that give rise to inequities in communities. The political dimension of service learning curricula must therefore engage in examining the complex social and institutional functions. "Citizenship requires that individuals work to *create, evaluate, criticize,* (italics ours), and change public institutions and programs" (Kahne and Westheimer, 597).

Teacher education scholarship must open up spaces for a critical analysis of education that challenges the way schools work with such issues as social difference, power relations and hierarchies, the distribution and use of community resources, and whose interests schools serve and who are marginalized (Hones 1997; O'Grady 2000).

Civic responsibility in the service learning and community development model must generate action. Teacher education is invariably critiqued for its pre-occupation with the "reflective" when "deep reflection can only occur when students have something meaningful upon which to reflect" (Tellez, Hlebowitsh, Cohen and Harwood 1995, 66). They urge educators to move from such a rhetoric to active social amelioration to promote "the kind of teacher who will work in the interests of culturally diverse and low income youth" (66).

As teachers' work becomes more complex because of the diversity within the schools and the communities they serve, critics urge teacher educators to build into their curriculum and pedagogy an approach that moves pre-service teachers out of practicum classrooms and schools and into communities that hone and nurture students' lives. Such community field experiences help teachers to "view pupils not as isolated individuals in classroom, but as members of total family and community environments" (Zeichner and Melnick 1996, 176).

The literature reveals the variety of pre-service teacher involvement in community-based projects and a range of organizational arrangements for their involvement. Those teachers in the Tellez et al. (1995) study of social service field experiences and teacher education were engaged with agencies such as the Salvation Army evening English as a Second Language (ESL) program, Big Brothers/Big Sisters, the urban YMCA after-school programs, and community health centres. In the Narode, Rennie-Hill, and Peterson (1994) urban community study, pre-service teachers performed services such as tutoring, counselling and coaching with social agencies, schools, churches, and homes. This study also investigated the community expectations of their schools and revealed people's perceptions, hopes and problems. It concludes: "The lack of communication between community members and school authorities was considered the main cause of harmful, prejudicial beliefs in students, parents, [school] administrators, and teachers" (17).

The structure and organizational arrangements of community involvement projects for pre-service teachers varied. In some projects, participants had the option of choosing their own project or selecting from a list of social service agencies (Tellez et al. 1995). Zeichner's (1996) study reveals a range of field experience options available to pre-service teachers. These include an optional human services project for a *School and Community* course; completion of practicum in schools serving ethnic and language minority students; cultural immersion experience including community service work in a minority community.

Most projects lay out specific requirements of the experience such as the intensity and duration of the community placement, the level of field supervision, recording and reporting formats, and grading systems. In some programs, compensating time was made available to participants whose projects were scheduled after school hours and on weekends.

Guadarrama (2000) concludes that without a service learning component, "teacher education lacks the capability of effectively educating teacher candidates in the richness and complexity of the community and its integral relationship to the inconsistencies in quality in the schooling practices of students" (228-229).

To summarize, a synthesis of the research literature on community involvement for pre-service teachers highlights essential principles, practices and outcomes such as:

- community involvement links the social and cultural foundations of education to critical analysis of schooling, civic responsibility and community action;
- teacher participants in community development projects are more likely to embark on culturally relevant pedagogy in their classrooms and schools. Exposure to different cultural realities guides teachers to structure learning to particular cultural contexts (Zeichner, 1996);
- experiential teacher education helps participants examine their personal views and attitudes towards others, correct harmful and prejudicial assumptions, and dispel myths about those who are "different";
- sustained interaction with the community provides an audit of community resources and needs. It helps to identify community partners (social services personnel, cultural experts) that schools can utilize in educating its students;
- to fulfil the learning objectives of community involvement projects, i.e. observing, planning intervention and sustained meaningful action, placements should be long term, not a passing tourist visit.

The initiatives that follow incorporate, to varying degrees, the above principles and practices.

PROGRAM DESIGN AND IMPLEMENTATION

Teacher candidates' community involvement initiatives were developed as an extension of the school and classroom practica where candidates spend over 60 percent of their teacher education. Prior to or during the initial stages of field involvement candidates get a theoretical and methodological orientation to community fieldwork.

Through Foundations of Education courses, candidates are introduced to the social, cultural, political and economic forces in the larger community that impact the pedagogical process. Because education ought to be a democratic process and progressive schools are inextricably linked to the communities they serve, it is imperative that teachers develop a strong professional relationship with these communities. Such partnerships must be based on first hand knowledge of the community, its needs, resources, and challenges.

Program design must include a methodological orientation to community study and involvement that includes such basic research skills as:

- seeking out reliable background knowledge of the demographic of the community, its racial and ethnocultural make-up, residential neighbourhoods, housing styles and provisions (e.g., single homes, high-rise apartments, government-assisted, etc.) and community services;
- observation skills and theoretical knowledge to identify ways in which the interaction of social, cultural, political and economic factors impact the schooling process;
- interview skills to ensure the representation of diverse voices in the community;
- bracketing assumptions about communities to ensure some level of objectivity when interacting with the community;
- exploring and auditing the resources of the community, its history, culture, and artifacts as curriculum resources for a culturally-relevant pedagogy.

This orientation to the theoretical and methodological understanding of community involvement is followed by entry into the community to identify some of the most urgent needs that can be realistically addressed by the candidates during their tenure at their practicum school. Community needs and resources are identified by (a) conducting exploratory observational research in the community, and (b) engaging in discussions with students, parents, community groups, social service agencies, teachers, school administrators, school council members and other stakeholders. From such sources of knowledge, candidates can then identify an area of need they can adequately address given their time frame and the available resources that these communities have to share.

Community initiatives are designed for candidates who will work in teams ranging from dyad partnerships to practicum school cohort groups that reflect the diversity of the population in the communities they engage. Guidelines for community involvement include the number of hours per month in the field (i.e. 6 hrs.). Compensating time is arranged for candidates who engage in activities after school hours and on weekends.[3] A community-involvement supervisor is provided by the teacher education program to help monitor, regulate and document activities in the initiative and to provide progress reports to teacher educators in the program. Candidates document their own experiences in journals and provide reflections on these experiences on an ongoing basis.

REFLECTIONS

Over the periods 1994–1996 and 2001–2002, over 158 teacher candidates participated in the Urban Diversity Teacher Education Program mandatory dimension of learning to teach.[4] The findings that follow reflect the range of community activities in which they were engaged and provide insights into ways in which the school, family and the community interact to produce positive social and educational outcomes. In their own narratives, candidates describe the challenges of working with children, youths and adults, especially those from ethnocultural minority communities, new immigrants making the complex adjustments to Canadian life, and those with social and economic problems.

Categories of Community Involvement
The range of community projects in which candidates were involved can be categorized as health and safety, social, cultural, recreational, academic, and political (see Table 7.2).

Some of the activities in Table 7.2 were initiated in the school and community by teacher candidates. But to a large extent candidates engaged with a number of social service agencies already in existence in the communities served by their practicum schools. They served with and were guided by experienced professionals in such disciplines as child care, social work, youth work, and community development.

Experiencing the Field
The extended reflections in this section represent the range of issues with which candidates engaged and their interpretations of these experiences. Issues include institutional impediments to youth empowerment; racial identity development and young children; presumptions about inner-city youth and

Table 7.2
Community involvement projects

Category	Activity/Program
Academic:	Mentoring, remedial work, ESL teaching, homework club, adult learning centre
Health and Safety:	Breakfast club, snack programs, winter attire provision programs, therapy assistance
Recreational:	Extra-curricular sports, dance clubs, youth art classes, coaching
Cultural:	Cultural heritage programs, new citizenship preparation classes, heritage languages, community radio, Girl Guides
Social:	Drop-in programs for youths "at risk"; community living leadership training, distress centre crisis management
Political:	Activity recruitment of the under-represented parents in school decision making (school councils); parent empowerment in school meetings

the potential impact of relationship building; teachers' ethnic identity and its impact on ethnic students; and questions of immigrant status, race and national identity. In the reflections that follow, candidates' narrations concerning their field experiences are followed by their analyses of the issue. Their frameworks for analysis often reflect the theories covered in their social and cultural Foundations of Education courses.

Reflection 1: Youth disempowerment at a multi [social] service centre

> As I sit in on the Youth Action Committee meetings, I am amazed to see the level of commitment of the youth that attend. These young people are discussing issues at a level that is not reached in many university courses. They are not facts or theories from books, but personal, daily experiences. There is a great deal of passion, frustration and anger.
>
> Themes from articles we had discussed in university class reappear in real situations. One youth mentions that it is essential that they learn how to talk and present themselves in a way that demands respect (cf. Lisa Delpit's code of power). The adult in the group takes a second seat and lets the youth lead the discussion. In many ways, I feel that the forum of discussion is similar to the "culture circles" described by Paulo Freire. People are encouraged to discuss their situations and,

from their discussions, come up with a plan of action. The role of the group leader is truly to facilitate discussion and ask the occasional question as necessary.

There have been lengthy discussions about difficult encounters with the police, educators and the media in regard to unfair stereotypes of visible minority youth and members of a low income housing community. A meeting with a community liaison officer from the neighbouring police division was truly disappointing. The officer in question had an answer for every experience or complaint brought up by the youth. He simply replied that he could not comment on this or that situation because he was not there. His tone was patronizing, condescending; he was deaf to any of the issues brought to the forum. Basically, his message was, "We're just doing our job."

Coming together as a group to discuss issues and meeting with members of community agencies does not mean that your voice will be heard when so many ears, hearts and minds are closed.

I wonder if youth's questions will ever be truly heard. Is there hope for change? I write this as the child of English immigrants, one who has spent some time in Central America. I have attended the weekly meetings of this multi-service centre—which is located in a subsidized housing development. Here, people are no strangers to poverty, unemployment, social welfare and drug trafficking; here police visits are fairly common.

The responses of the youth themselves vary greatly. Some feel that education of people who hold racist ideas, and anti-racist education for young children from dominant backgrounds will be the answer. Others feel that nothing will change. However, they too continue to attend meetings on a bi-weekly basis.

Often I feel that it is the fear of retaliation that causes people to remain silent. In a 'democratic' world, one would never think that speaking up meant becoming vulnerable to those in power. However, this is reality for many of the youth and their families. It seems like a vicious trap. People gather together to discuss issues; they speak up to demand that changes occur; they face some form of "punishment," however covert, for speaking up; so they resolve to remain quiet, refusing to have hope and thus be burned again.

(Jane, Class of '95)

Reflection 2: The politics of transformative education for "ethnic" youth

"We want to learn about our history, our literature. We blame the education system. It has always reflected the inequalities of the larger society in classrooms. The curriculum has been set up for the sake of political expediency." These were the words of militancy that I heard at a Latin-American Youth group meeting.

For the community involvement program, I had chosen to do volunteer work in the Latin-American community. I was born in South America and felt I would have an affinity with them. Soon I learned that little was being done to help these students to succeed academically. Their community leaders and parents need to find out about the education system, how it functions, and how decisions are made.

(Juanita, Class of '95)

Reflection 3: Racial identity in the Parents and Tots program

I am Italo-Canadian and my dyad partner is of Chinese descent. Together we developed this program to meet a need in an inner-city community of newcomers to Canada from the Caribbean, South and Central America, former communist European countries and the Philippines. Our aim was to stimulate the children's social, emotional, physical, intellectual, cultural and creative growth, to provide a regular weekly opportunity for parents to meet and share ideas, concerns and aspirations with one another and constructive time with their children.

Incident

It was near the end of our "Pre-school Fun" program (ages 2 to 5) and my partner and I had sung our good-bye song. After that, we offered the parents some refreshments while the children played amongst themselves under the supervision of the mothers. A black boy (age 3) became cranky and approached his [black] mother, saying that he wanted to go home. His mother said, "Sh!" and gave him a lollipop since she was conversing with another [white] mother. The boy's mother asked the white mother if her daughter (age 3) would like a lollipop as well. The white mother said no. After a few minutes, the boy turned around to the girl and gave her the lollipop to lick. As the white child licked the lollipop, I noticed the tense and shocked looks on their mothers' faces as they gazed at the children. I froze when I saw the mothers' expressions.

Then the boy's mother turned to the other mother and said, "I'm sorry, I'll go and take the lollipop away." The girl's mother gazed away from the children and looked the black mother in the face. I thought for sure that she was going to get angry, but all she said was, "No, I'm sorry for not accepting the lollipop when you offered it. I did not want to spoil her lunch." After the girl's mother said this, I saw relief in the face of the black mother. After the two mothers left, I was approached by another mother (Latino) who had seen the incident and she said, "I'm relieved that nothing came out of that incident. Can you imagine the negative effect it would have had on the two children if they had witnessed their mothers fighting?" I thought about the incident for several days and I am glad I have the opportunity to talk about it.

Theme: Racial Identity Development of Young Children.

Question underlying the theme: What does this lollipop incident tell us about racial identity development?

The factors contributing to identity formation can include a child's ethnicity, race personal family influences, geographic origin (e.g. prairie, rural), religious background, gender, economic class, age, and ability. This lollipop incident has shown me that a child's attitudes are shaped by their parental attitudes towards different racial groups. According to Helene and Ahmed Ijaz in the article *Racial Attitudes and Identity,* the societal and individual attitudes children encounter about their race and other races may have a significant impact upon their racial/cultural identity and self-esteem. From observing the way the white mother responded to the incident, I would say that she "affirms a positive racial/cultural identity in her child by emphasizing the equal value of people of all races and cultures." Young children can be damaged intellectually, socially, and emotionally if their parents fail to provide them with authentic and balanced images of people belonging to diverse racial and ethnocultural groups. By receiving unrealistic, distorted images of other people, children are also receiving distorted images of themselves and a false sense of their relationship with others. This could have happened if the two mothers had argued over their sharing of the lollipop.

At another session, several mothers commented favourably on our use of multicultural books which depict diversity in race, ethnicity, gender, physical abilities and occupations. They asked us why all teachers do not use such books, since they have elementary school-age children.

I described our Urban Diversity Teacher Education Program and its emphasis on anti-discriminatory pedagogy. The mothers believe that children should learn about their culture and the cultures of others in the school. If children are taught to recognize and appreciate the diversity of cultures while they are young, then they will continue to live in harmony with others when they become adults. They may encounter resistance, prejudice and racist attitudes along the way, but they will not be easily swayed. Thus, anti-racist attitudes must be taught and modelled by parents in the home as well as teachers in school. We cannot blame a child for what we teach them. As adults, we have a social responsibility to try to identify and deal with the prejudice and racism inherent in the environment. I want to empower my students to be change-agents so they can work to change this prevalent power position (e.g., occupational advantage due to race, gender, class). With the cooperative effort of parents and teachers, we can work to make this happen. Anti-racist learning must begin in the home with parents and continue in the school with teachers. Parental attitudes and upbringing can often affect a child's racial identity development.

(Mary, Class of '95)

Reflection 4: Troublesome assumptions at "Street Level" Drop-in Centre

When I walked into "Street Level" which is a drop-in centre for youth ages 13 to 18, to help with the tutoring program I was quite nervous and uncomfortable. What I saw were small groups of teenagers either were playing pool, video games, ping-pong, or watching television. Others were just sitting, staring blankly at no one in particular. Although the staff seemed friendly enough, I felt quite out of place, being the only East Asian in the whole centre. I did not know whether I should attempt to talk to the members or just observe. Only one youth acknowledged my presence, but only because the coordinator introduced her to me. I felt quite invisible and out of place; I felt as if I could not relate to what they were doing. I expected some of them to be reading, doing homework, or at least talking about school. When I asked the coordinator how the tutoring program had fared, he said, "Dismally. They just aren't interested at all." There was also no interest in the dozens of books I saw on the shelves, or anything related to school. Being a teacher at heart, I was quite baffled and wondered what I was going to do for these youths who had such little interest in school or anything in its likeness. I was taken aback at the foul language that was spoken, out of earshot of the staff, as well as the 'rough' way in which they interacted with each other. As a teacher candidate in the primary/junior school division, I did not know how to react to these teenagers with an "attitude".

I was wrong to make these assumptions. As the months went by, I learned a lot about myself as well as the youth members.

Reflection upon Assumptions

Assumptions often hinder establishing positive relationships between teachers and students.

I realize that the discomfort I felt at the beginning and the assumptions I had formed, e.g. that these students were unmotivated to do school work because of their apparent lack of effort, were crucial to my development as a teacher entering an unfamiliar setting. I am beginning to understand the harmful nature of assumptions and the biases that stem from them. The more time I spent at the Centre, the more I began to empathize with the students in their hostility to teachers and school. At first I saw them as the ones with the 'problem'. I was challenged to reflect on ways in which we can improve the educational system, motivate youth who seem so lost and disaffected, and share the decision-making power with staff and students. The students often looked bored and depressed. As I met with them over time, I learned that they had the same needs as students have always had, that is, to feel listened to, to have a communicative link with people who care and do not condescend. Teachers who practise the humanizing pedagogy of students as subjects rather than objects, believe that cooperative effort can make a difference. The future will be bleak for youth if the school system does not acknowledge them as important stake-holders who have sensible ideas to contribute. This year the Urban Diversity Program introduced me to critical issues of culture and race. I have become determined to use that knowledge for the better understanding and improvement of others' life conditions.

(Susan, Class of '95)

Reflection 5: The practice of freedom

There may be hope for these students. There may be hope for the other marginalized sectors of Canadian society. But this will come about only through the constant demand of parents and community leaders for school officials and trustees to be accountable to, and serve the interests of all their constituents. Only in this way will the school system be made aware of the inequity that exists in its midst.

Meanwhile, as an educator I will always keep in mind Shaull's words "there is no such thing as a neutral education process. Education either functions as an instrument which is used to facilitate the integration of the younger generation into the logic of the present system and bring about conformity in it, or it becomes 'the practice of freedom,' the means by which men and women deal critically and creatively with reality and discover how to participate in the transformation of their world." (Richard Shaull, Foreword to Paulo Freire's *Pedagogy of the oppressed*, New York, 1973, p. 15).

There is hope as long as youth such as this militant Latin-American youngster [in his Community Involvement project] continue to give evidence of an ability to deal critically with reality; as long as they demonstrate a readiness to discover ways to participate in the transformation of their world and can convince others within their community that self-help is the activating force of progress.

(John, Class of '95)

Reflection 6: Moving beyond judgments and stereotypes

My involvement in the [Afghan] association helped me to know the Afghan people better. So this experience enriched my personal knowledge. It also helped me professionally, because I am sure I will meet Afghan children where I teach and now I feel more comfortable dealing with them. I can relate to them better and understand their difficulties in the educational system (e.g. with English I know that they have a different alphabet; girls didn't go to school in Afghanistan during the Taliban regime so they miss some very important skills when they came here). So basically, I had a chance to explore the real lives of my student outside the classroom and create a culturally relevant pedagogy that will meet their individual needs.

I saw many Afghani refugees and immigrants in my country (because Afghanistan is a neighbour of Iran). I do not know why but in Iran the majority of these refugees and immigrants are poor, uneducated and are believed to be "social undesirables." We were always taught by our parents to keep our distance from them and be careful. That was the main reason that I was hesitant to go to the Afghan community here in Toronto; frankly speaking, I was scared of them. However, I took a risk and chose the Afghan community as my placement. The first day I went there, I was quite surprised because I saw many well-behaved, educated and kind Afghanis who were completely different than those I saw in my country. While talking to some of them, I found out they all have post-secondary degrees, and they are very respectful people; they all are immigrants and have been here for a short time (I mean they are not the product of Canada). Now, I am confessing my mistake because I pre-judged the Afghan people. From the time that I have been in the Afghan community, I have talked about Afghan people to my family and friends and I try to clarify for them that not all Afghanis are like the Afghani immigrants in Iran or Talibans! Participating in this community involvement program provided me many insightful experiences; the most important one was to not pre-judge people, because not being judgmental is the most important characteristic that a teacher should have in order to provide a neutral and fair learning environment.

(Marge, Class of '01)

Reflection 7: Immigrant forever!

Our proposal to the *Third World Association* to tutor their children was well received. Over the months enrolment increased as we employed a number of teaching strategies.

But it was the informal talks with the students that provided me with the opportunity to talk about race and culture. In one such discussion, a student reported that someone at school had told her that a person had to be white to be a Canadian and that she could not be a Canadian. On further investigation, I found out that they were uncertain whether or not they were Canadian. To my astonishment, when I presented them with a scenario of several immigrants from various parts of the world who were now living in Canada, they confirmed that only the person of European ancestry was Canadian. As a naturalized Canadian who was born in the West Indies, I was disturbed.

The question: Who exactly is Canadian?

Immigrant children living in Canada need to be made aware of their status as Canadians. They need to be made to feel that they belong. The fact that they are recent immigrants seems already to set them up for the feeling that they are visitors. It is important for them to realize that, once their parents have taken the necessary steps for them to become naturalized citizens, then they have the right to call themselves Canadian if they so desire. The crucial issue is not what they choose to call themselves, but what influenced their decision to arrive at that chosen identification.

These immigrant children may be quite satisfied with identifying themselves as Jamaicans, Haitians, Somalians, Trinidadians, Ethiopians or Barbadians, but what about the next generation that is born in Canada? Will they feel the same alienation from the mainstream of Canadian society because of their skin colour? This may well be the case, because I think the underlying issue is not so much one of place of origin but one of resemblance; resemblance to European physiognomy.

(Pauline, Class of '95)

To summarize, candidates' insightful reflections upon their community experiences focus attention on the struggle for equity, social justice and democratic life. Reflections 1 and 2 raise questions about the dialectical relationships that exist between institutional power vested in law enforcement agents and school agents on the one hand, and on the other, marginalized youth and ethnic communities. Dialogical processes intended to build trust and positive relationships across borders end up in reticence on the part of law enforcement agents and "silence" from inner-city, racial minority youth. Candidates working with these community groups gain valuable insights into the impediments to democratic dialogue across "borders", and raise challenging pedagogical questions of race, social class and power in the schooling process.

The question of race and ethnic identity in educational institutions is pervasive in the remaining reflections. Candidates explored the tensions and contradictions of serving in multicultural, multiracial communities and the uncertainties of cross-race encounters among children and their parents. In their sustained involvement with inner-city, racial minority youth, candidates interrogated their own stereotypic assumptions and relocated blame for these students' academic underachievement to school curriculum and pedagogy. These field experiences reaffirm the notion of providing culturally relevant pedagogy for children from diverse communities (Ladson-Billings 1995).

SOME CHALLENGES OF COMMUNITY INVOLVEMENT

Teacher candidates' engagement with the community is not without its challenges. In a less controlled learning environment than traditional teacher education, and with less predictability of learning process and outcomes, emerging obstacles must be perceived as challenges to be overcome. In the section that follows, we discuss some of the issues that surfaced during candidates' community action and offer suggestions for working constructively with those obstacles.

A rather conservative stance taken by some practicum school administrators is that candidates should not actively engage in "political work." This is in response to candidates outreach to community members who have not traditionally participated in the schooling process. These are the working class and the poor, racial and ethnic minorities, and recent immigrants that are marginalized by institutions such as schools; they have not adequately represented themselves or their children's interests, and have not been perceived as equal or contributing members of the schooling process.[5] O'Grady (2000) confirms this tendency for teacher education to be seen as a pedagogical process and the service learning dimension as a philosophy and pedagogy devoid of political influence. Here she expresses the importance of teachers' political positioning and civic responsibility:

> Because education is "contested territory," in which the relations between interest, conflict, and power are perpetually being played out ... teachers who do not specifically explicate political positions can neither teach students the meanings of *e pluribus unum* nor help students understand the political dimensions of civic responsibility. It is imperative that the analysis of structural politics in education be as rigorous as the analysis of any other aspect of education if educators hope to help students identify possibilities for change. (O'Grady 2000, 11)

It is essential that educators, even at the pre-service stage, start to perceive their work for equity, social justice and democratic schooling as a political process. Any struggle for representation of "voice" in institutional settings must necessarily be political. Candidate advocacy and the redistribution of power among those who, because of their conditions of life, have been absent from the table will make the educational process a more equitable one. Hartnett and Carr (1995) perceive teachers' role to be "critical pivots between the state, parental power, institutional power and the development of democratic values and attitudes in each new generation" (43). Pre-service teachers must therefore be empowered in their community-oriented teacher education to support parents and their communities by actively seeking out voices that are traditionally under-represented in the schooling process.

Community Involvement as Extra Work in Unfamiliar Contexts

A concern of some candidates is that community involvement is an additional burden carried out in communities outside of their "comfort zones." They argue that volunteerism with children and youth in schools and communities was already a prerequisite for entry into teacher education. A second concern is their request to engage in projects in their own neighbourhoods instead of communities in which their practicum schools are located.

Our response to the first issue is that candidates perceive community action more as learning than service (Howard 1993). This dimension of teacher education should be articulated as an extension of, and integrated into, the social and cultural foundations of education courses as well as classroom practica. Academic credits are earned for learning, for a critical analysis of praxis, and for generating new theories about the process of community involvement as learning to teach. This academic approach moves well beyond volunteerism in which candidates may have been engaged prior to their teacher education.

This links to the issue of involvement context. Some candidates request placements in their own home communities for logistical and "comfort" reasons. They argue for the ease with which they can access, identify with, and work with schools, social services agencies and recreational programs in neighbourhoods in which they live. Obviously, they feel safer in these communities (See Cochran-Smith, 2000 for similar concerns of teacher candidates she studied). But knowledge of candidates' home locations reveals that, to a large extent, they reside in middle-class, suburban communities that reflect their own racial, ethnocultural and social class identities. Involvement in "communities of difference" provides the steepest learning curve for candidates.

For many, this may well be their first and only structured, sustained exposure to working-class, inner-city and immigrant communities, and such an exposure provides the opportunity for candidates to actively foster school-community linkages as a response to needs of the community and, in turn, prepare themselves to offer a culturally relevant pedagogy.

To conclude, we draw on Kinsley and McPherson's (1995) description of some broader challenges to community service learning cited in O'Grady (2000, 12). Community involvement must address real social justice issues and must not be trivialized or routinized. In addition, there must be a true collaboration with the community to avoid paternalism. If field-based learning is not theoretically linked, it can easily strengthen rather than weaken stereotypes. O'Grady warns, "service learning can too easily reinforce oppressive outcomes. It can perpetuate racist, sexist, or classist assumptions about others and reinforce a colonialist mentality of superiority" (12).

IMPLICATIONS FOR TEACHER EDUCATION

This study of pre-service teachers and their sustained involvement in the community provides insights into the benefits of such initiatives to the candidates and the schools and communities in which they learn to teach. Candidates learn about the social, cultural and economic factors of community that influence children's lives. More importantly, they engage the community in ways that develop the resources to fulfill the needs of its citizens. By engaging the community, candidates gain valuable insights into their own needs to grow personally and professionally. At the personal level, they learn to interrogate their own identity development and its potential impact on their perceptions and responses to the very diverse world around them. At the professional level, their involvement in the community prepares them for engaging in culturally relevant pedagogy in the classroom.

But community involvement as teacher education pedagogy is not without its challenges. We see from this study that there is a perception that community engagement should be restricted to the moral and intellectual domains. That is, relationships would emphasize charity or giving (the moral domain), and experience-based learning would foster higher order thinking (intellectual domain) (Kahne and Westheimer 1996). Conservative elements critiqued any political engagement with the community (by facilitating participation in the schooling of the children) as inappropriate for the curriculum of teacher education.

The other challenges emerging from this study are (a) candidates' discomfort about working in unfamiliar socio-economic and cultural contexts (i.e., inner-city schools and communities with which they are unfamiliar), and (b) providing "service" beyond the parameters of the school day. These are issues that must be addressed in the conceptualization and the putting into operation of service learning programs in teacher education.

The following quote from Kahne and Westheimer (1996, 597) summarizes very succinctly the way service learning ought to be conceptualized and put into practice:

Many contemporary scholars focus on change over charity and argue that the lack of connection between individual rights and communal obligations within our culture has left us with a bankrupt sense of citizenship... [M]any current service activities emphasize altruism and charity and fail to call into question current notions of individualism or to encourage the type of political participation that furthers democracy.

The challenges are many for those planning to move teacher education beyond university lecture-rooms and practicum classrooms into the community. From the findings of this study and others reported in the research literature, there appear to be two essential dimensions of community involvement and teacher education: (1) conceptualizing and linking community involvement curriculum with the social and cultural foundations theory of schooling, and (2) providing the structural arrangements to utilize the curriculum.

(1) *Conceptualizing community involvement*

Schools and the communities they serve are inextricably linked. For schools to serve communities better, teacher preparation programs must engage their participants in examining the relationships between schools and communities, the socio-cultural and political underpinnings of such relationships, whose interests are best served by schools, how resources are distributed, what community groups have voice, power privilege in schools and what groups are marginalized.

Linking theoretical course work with experiential community involvement helps teachers to construct meanings from their experiences—meanings that will subsequently help them to develop a culturally relevant curriculum that will guide their pedagogy. A community-involvement model based on change, social amelioration and social reconstruction must examine the conditions of life in these communities, the historical background to such conditions and the ways that such conditions are reproduced. Most importantly, such a change model must develop strategies for disrupting the reproduction cycle.

A new conception of community involvement must be adopted that examines how democratic values are taken up in educational institutions and that applies the principles of equity, diversity and social justice to the examination of educational processes and community participation in these processes. Community action guided by this conceptual framework brings a critical inquiry approach to experiential learning.

(2) *Providing programmatic structures*

Effective community involvement requires collaboration with practicum schools, social service agencies, and other vested interest groups within the community. Entry points for pre-service teachers must be strategically worked out so that communities perceive and accept them as learners and helpers.

Candidates must be provided with guidelines to conduct their own investigations into community needs and resources, following the process of needs and resource assessment; prioritizing from a hierarchy of needs based on time and available resources to effect change; developing a plan of action; and implementing the plan to achieve the desired change (Kahne and Westheimer 1996; Tellez et al. 1995; Zeichner 1996). The implementation phase requires a structure for monitoring, providing feedback, and documentation. A communication system is required that facilitates open discourse between all players (teacher candidates, teacher educators and supervisors, practicum school representatives, social service agents and other community partners). With such a structure in place, these groups would certainly benefit from this initiative in teacher education. Utilizing the mentor teacher as partner in the teacher-as-researcher process would provide a dimension of help from an experienced practitioner.

To conclude, the community involvement approach has interesting implications for teacher education. It interrogates traditional conceptions and practices, and offers instead an approach that is collaborative, experiential, praxis driven, and socially reconstructive. Most of all, it opens up possibilities for education as a democratic process—a connection between education and democracy that philosophers perceive as intrinsic (Carr and Hartnett 1996; Levin 2000). Community involvement makes teacher education truly responsive to the needs of the community it serves.

ENDNOTES

1. There are ongoing debates over the "marketization" of schooling and the growing involvement of the private sector through partnerships and multi-stakeholder collaboration. To explore these issues further, see J.P. Portelli and R.P. Solomon (eds.). (2001), *The erosion of democracy in education: Critique to possibilities.*

2. There may well be differences in the way these terms are conceptualized and practiced. For example, see Schecter, Solomon and Kittner (2003). In this chapter, the following terms that are similar in meaning and practice will be used interchangeably: service learning, community experiential learning, community field experience, and community involvement.

3. Compensating time cannot be "banked" or accumulated to be claimed at a later time. This would seriously disrupt the continuity of the practicum experience within classrooms. Hours for "time back" must be taken in the month that they are earned.

4. All (70) TCs in the 2000–2001 cohort participated in an extensive study of the needs of the community served by their practicum school, and developed an action plan for change (similar to the exploratory work done by Narode, Rennie-Hill and Peterson 1994). This awareness study was a part of the Social and Cultural Foundations of Education course and did not have an implementation component.

5. The non-involvement of some groups arises from their assumptions about the school process. Groups such as immigrants from cultures that perceive the educational process as the business of the school and the teacher as "expert," tend to relinquish their roles as partners in the educational process. Others such as the working class are marginalized because they feel, or are made to feel, inadequate in representing their interests in the bureaucratic structures of schools.

chapter eight

The Professional Development School as a "Community of Learners"

INTRODUCTION

Part I of this book provides a damning critique of the process of teacher development and its limited potential to be transformative. In such a critique, teacher preparation institutions and local school board PD personnel that engage in pre-service and in-service work were seriously implicated for their lack of creativity and synergy in providing new structural arrangements for progressive work. This resulted in the discontinuity of teacher learning from the university lecture room to the practicum classroom and, as well, PD for in-service practitioners was often perceived to be sporadic, discontinuous and impeded by teacher workload and competing interests. How then may teacher educators and those institutions responsible for teacher development collaborate in providing better learning environments for teachers?

In this final chapter, we introduce the concept of professional development schools (PDS) as learning environments where teacher candidates, veteran practitioners and teacher educators work together as a "community of learners." Such schools (also labelled "professional practice schools," "laboratory schools," and "clinical schools" [from the medical model of preparing medical practitioners]) have been promoted as sites that transform the teaching-learning environment and the education of children. The institutional arrangements for PDSs would be school-university partnerships—Faculties of Education within university settings that would develop formal or informal collaborative arrangements with school districts or individual schools for the purpose of transforming classroom pedagogy.

The objectives of this chapter are to provide a critical review of PDSs and the ways they have been conceptualized and put into practice in various school jurisdictions. From this synthesis we will present alternative model designs that have proven effective in preparing teachers to work equitably with the growing diversity in our schools and communities, and the logistical challenges they face in implementation.

CONCEPTUALIZING THE PDS

The concept of professional development schools emerged from teacher education reform ideas of the Holmes Group (later renamed the Holmes Partnership) in the United States in the 1980s and 1990s. This consortium of higher educational research institutions recommended, among other things, that designated schools become "clinical sites" and sites of inquiry for teacher candidates. The Holmes Group also recommended a more cohesive and integrated teacher education, through the collaborative efforts of colleges of education and the school system. Since then the research literature has provided an impressive list of expectations, principles, practices, and challenges for PDSs.

The consensus of researchers is that most PDS initiatives appear to have four main functions:

- the preparation of teacher candidates;
- the professional development of in-service teachers;
- research and inquiry into teaching and learning; and
- the improvement of student learning and experiences (Levine and Churins 1999; Clarke 1999; Schwartz 2000).

Conceptualizing the PDS as a clinical setting, Levine and Churins advocate for a better articulation between campus-based and school-based components of teacher education programs; a site where theory and practice are interfaced; a collaboration of school and university forming a hybrid institution for teacher development. Their argument:

> Teacher learning—from novice to experienced teacher—should occur in the direct context of teaching. And the corollary: When teachers are learners, their students' learning is enhanced. In other words, new teacher learning, professional development, student learning, and research are all bound together. (1999,195)

Key for this chapter is Levine and Churins' charting of the four PDS functions and the ways such critical attributes as learning community, collaboration, accountability and quality assurance, organization, roles and structure, and equity relate to each (196-197). With a focus on the attribute of equity, each PDS function clearly articulates the objectives to be achieved (see Table 8.1 below).

Table 8.1
PDS functions and the attribute of equity

Function	Attribute: Equity
Teacher education	School and university curricula reflect diversity and are non-discriminatory
	Opportunities to learn are equitably supported
Staff development	PDS is characterized by norms and practices which support equity and learning by all students and adults
	Opportunities to learn are equitably supported
Practice-based inquiry	School and university faculty engage families and communities in support of student learning
Student learning	Interns (teacher candidates) work with children with diverse needs
	Opportunities to learn are equitably supported

Table 8.1 is adapted from Table 4: "How the critical attributes pertain to each of the PDS functions," in Marsha Levine and Eleanor Churins (1999). Designing standards that empower professional development schools. *Peabody Journal of Education*, 74: 3, 4, 178-208.

From the research literature we have summarized some of the benefits of PDS for teacher candidates:

- the chance to put theory into practice in actual field experiences. An ongoing concern for teacher candidates in the traditional practicum setting is the lack of opportunity to implement theories learned in university lecture-rooms;
- the chance to work collaboratively as one of many members of a PDS. This is a distinct move away from the "apprenticeship model" with a one-on-one relationship between a mentor teacher and teacher candidate;

- candidates are likely to experience greater success when PDSs "avoid the inexcusable practice... of assigning beginning teachers full time responsibilities in the most challenging setting with nominally, if any, informed assistance from others" (Howey 1999, 328); and
- the opportunity to learn and integrate field-based inquiry into the teaching-learning process; to learn the practice of "teacher-as-researcher" assessing the needs of students, their families and communities, and developing an action plan for change.

Benefits of the PDS for in-service teachers include:

- the opportunity to become a better "reflective practitioner." Lieberman and Miller (1990) argue that a dynamic PDS environment with university scholars and teacher candidates infusing new ideas into the setting is likely to help veteran teachers replace routinized practices with reflective action in their curriculum and instruction; and
- the opportunity of collegiality with "colleagues-in-training." Lieberman and Miller (1990) found that veteran teachers increase their self-examination, risk-taking and collective reflection upon practice when placed in a collaborative relationship with other professionals. They assert:

> Traditions of privacy, practicality, and isolation were replaced by shared ownership of issues, and a desire to work together as colleagues... . These notions of shared work, shared problem-solving, mutual assistance, and teacher leadership in curriculum and instruction are, to our minds, the cornerstones of building a school culture that supports continuous inquiry into practice. (108)

- the opportunity for collaboration in teacher research and inquiry. Schools and classrooms become "centres of inquiry" when teachers engage in structured investigation into their practice. With the support and participation of teacher candidates and teacher educators, teacher practitioners can identify and investigate student problems, search for solutions, and experiment with new pedagogical approaches. Such a team approach to classroom inquiry provides the necessary time and support for practitioners to perceive themselves as "ground level" researchers generating useful research knowledge.

Benefits of PDS for teacher educators from the university setting include:

- replacement of lecture-dominated instruction with a more collaborative, inclusive structure that has more intrinsic rewards;
- chances to develop research that documents explicitly "the positive impact of PDS efforts on student learning" (Ross, Brownell, Sindelar, and Vandiver 1999, 220);
- relationships with teacher candidates and teacher practitioners in the field are established and have multiple visible and invisible lifelong benefits; and
- the limits to "expert" knowledge must be considered in the light of alternative "expert" research that is currently alive in many PDS models. According to Levine and Churins (1999, 201):

> Standards that are developed by 'experts' through the process of consensus may lack the authenticity that arises from the engagement with them in practice. Even the top-down and bottom-up approach we used in developing the draft standards falls short. We conclude that only by taking the draft standards to the field, where PDSs could work with them, could we determine if they were the "right" standards if they were useful.

Indeed, with pre-service candidates, in-service teachers and teacher educators all benefiting from school-university partnerships, the students, and their communities of origin, should be potential beneficiaries. Quinn and McKay's (1998, 7) research findings suggest that "a school culture can be changed through a partnership with a university, through focused teacher interactions, and through the assignment of a large number of student teachers to a single school." Howey (1999, 324) concludes, "The salient features of good schools, good teaching and learning, and in turn, good teacher education need to be repeatedly reinforced."

But what are the challenges to the PDS? What factors may restrict the repeated reinforcement mentioned above? The research literature cites a number of challenges that are structural, institutional, socio-cultural, and even ideological. Some specific challenges to the transformative agenda of PDS are: fear of change ("reform paralysis"); unwillingness to take risks; fear of overwork; feeling of disorientation during the early stages of PDS implementation; lack of resources and concerns over sustainability; communication problems; the complexity and time-consuming institutional differences between the school and the university; coordination of teacher preparation dimension, etc. (Johnston 1999; Levine and Churins 1999; Lieberman and Miller 1990; Ross et al. 1999; Tom 1999). Ross et al. conclude, "the impact on schools, children, and teacher education is minimal because social norms and patterns of practice within participating institutions do not change" (212). Lieberman and Miller (1990, 114) alluded to the challenges of schools making the "transition from bureaucratic and hierarchical modes of leadership to alternative forms."

For our model of the PDS as a "community of learners," we are informed by the research on institutional and pedagogical change:

> Large scale change, like that envisioned by the Holmes Group, will be harder to achieve. As an interim step, teachers and teacher

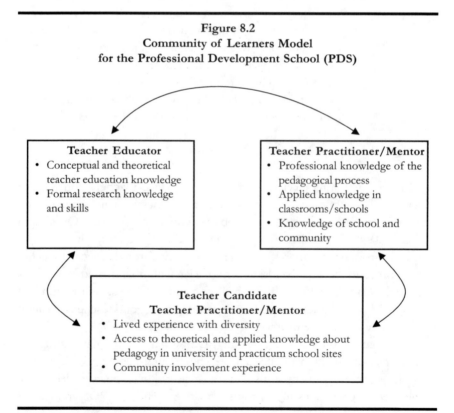

Figure 8.2
Community of Learners Model
for the Professional Development School (PDS)

Teacher Educator
- Conceptual and theoretical teacher education knowledge
- Formal research knowledge and skills

Teacher Practitioner/Mentor
- Professional knowledge of the pedagogical process
- Applied knowledge in classrooms/schools
- Knowledge of school and community

Teacher Candidate
Teacher Practitioner/Mentor
- Lived experience with diversity
- Access to theoretical and applied knowledge about pedagogy in university and practicum school sites
- Community involvement experience

Teaching for Equity and Diversity

educators may need smaller, more reasonable goals to work toward. (Ross et al. 1999, 217)

The model that we propose is guided by the advice of Ross et al.; it starts with a small cluster within the teacher education triad: the teacher educator, the teacher candidate and the teacher practitioner and mentor. Figure 8.2 documents the awareness, knowledge, experiences, skills, and resources that members of the triad bring to this community of learners. Even more important is the dynamic interrelationship and interdependence forged by the partners in their professional teaching and learning capacities. The theory-practice interface generated by this model provides a learning environment that is potentially equitable and diverse for all partners in the education process.

MODEL APPLICATION

The three school-based professional learning approaches outlined below evolved from the needs of teachers to grow as a community. Although their contexts, objectives, project design and implementation vary, the common themes running through these initiatives are teachers learning together to achieve some measure of educational equity and diversity in their pedagogy. In each initiative, the rationale, content and process will be outlined as well as the outcomes, the challenges and their implications for teacher development.

THE ETOBICOKE-UNIVERSITY PARTNERSHIP MODEL[1]

The rationale of the Etobicoke model was to engage in the process of simultaneous renewal of teachers at the in-service and pre-service levels with a focus on educational inclusivity and diversity. This design incorporates the following process and content:

A Non-evaluative PD Environment

This provides for a non-evaluative environment where veteran teachers, teacher candidates and teacher educators come together as a community of learners sharing their knowledge, experiences and practices of working effectively for school change.

Very often, the conservative cultures of schools dampen any enthusiasm and good intentions that TCs (teacher candidates) may bring to the classroom. The socio-political context of teaching prescribes a relationship among the triad: the TC, the cooperating teacher and the practicum supervisor (teacher-educator). Menter (1989) refers to this relationship as a culture that translates into teaching-practice stasis. "School... triads typically exhibit a property of stasis. All members of the triad seek to minimize, counteract or negate any influence or innovation which might upset the stability of the triad" (460). Maintaining such rigidly prescribed roles, responsibilities and the power relations of the triad restricts the promotion of equity and diversity in the classroom.

TCs feel intimidated about critiquing the curriculum and pedagogy taken for granted within schools, and are instead pressured to implement prepackaged curricula in practicum classrooms in a mechanical fashion (Liston and Zeichner 1991, 184). In such an environment, TCs experience personal frustrations, unfulfilled pedagogical objectives and limited professional growth (Menter 1989; Crozier and Menter 1993). Ultimately, students in practicum classrooms lose the benefit of multiple perspectives, knowledge, experiences and resources that TCs of varied racial and ethnocultural backgrounds may bring to the pedagogical process.

Indeed, utilizing a neutral, alternative PD site away from the potential restrictions of the practicum school provides some measure of freedom and security for all participants, especially for teacher candidates.

Inclusive Conceptual Model

We decided to implement an inclusive education conceptual model based on Peggy McIntosh's model of *Seeking Educational Equity and Diversity* (SEED). This model and its various adaptations have been utilized successfully in the critical inquiry into classroom practice and in helping teachers to develop strategies for implementing educational equity and diversity.

With the participation of 44 TCs from York's Urban Diversity Teacher Education Program, the cooperating teachers and principals from practicum schools in Etobicoke (Toronto, Ontario) and teacher educators from both institutions, a series of 7 half-day workshops[2] was offered from September 1995 to May 1996 covering such topics as: The Inclusive Curriculum: An Introduction; Gender Equity and Schooling; Issues of Equity and Ability; Race, Culture, Identity and Schooling; Race, Culture and the Media; Social Class and Schooling and Reflections: Revisiting Curriculum.

Prior to each session, workshop presenters provided background research materials relevant to their topic. Evaluations at the end of each workshop provided valuable feedback from participants on the effectiveness of the program and additional assessment of their professional development needs for future workshops.

Expressed Enthusiasm for the Veteran-New Teacher Interface

Both TCs and cooperating teachers expressed an appreciation for a non-evaluative environment where both groups shared current pedagogical ideas and concepts, extensive classroom practices and school-community experiences. The sharing of different points of view and the meaningful dialogues generated among participants was certainly a highlight of the program. This exchange was significant because half of the TCs in the Urban Diversity Program were of racial and ethnocultural minority backgrounds while their cooperating teachers were almost exclusively from the dominant culture.

Some Challenges

Provision of Theory-Practice Balance and Continuity

There is need for a workshop structure and progression (preferably a full-day session) that begins with a theoretical overview followed by small (integrated TC and cooperating teacher) group discussion. This should be followed by the examination of hands-on classroom materials and the collaborative development of specific lessons plans for classroom delivery. There must be a conscious and calculated effort by workshop facilitators to ensure integrated and collaborative small-group work among TCs, cooperating teachers and teacher educators.

Enlisting School Administrators as Agents of Change

This project confirms that genuine teacher commitment and involvement in educational equity and diversity issues are to a large extent dependent on their school administrators' active involvement. When administrators attended, teacher participation was good; when there was no administrative support, teachers gradually withdrew, claiming program irrelevance to their needs. Such a response may well be rooted partly in a deeper educator resistance to equity and diversity issues in Canadian schools (Solomon and Levine-Rasky 1996a). The biggest challenge of teacher educators and Boards of Education will be to ensure that the inclusive curriculum is central to leadership development programs. Only if these players work in synchrony can simultaneous renewal in both institutions be achieved.

THE MAPLE LEAF-UNIVERSITY
PARTNERSHIP MODEL[3]

Teaching Social Justice In Pre-Service Education Through Partnerships With Schools

This Maple Leaf professional development model for pre- and in-service teachers grew out of a partnership between Maple Leaf School, a practicum site, and York University. Significant players in this partnership were the school's administrative team, the school district's Anti-racism and Ethnocultural Unit coordinator, and the University's Practicum coordinator. The goal of this project was to facilitate the professional growth of teacher candidates in a practicum setting with a racially and ethnoculturally diverse student population.

According to Norquay (1996):

> This project at Maple Leaf School offered the possibility of forming a pedagogical and curricular partnership between university seminar and the school practicum placement in order to better address the issues around helping pre-service teachers become both committed and competent equity educators. (2)

Essential ingredients in the achievement of this goal were:

- an administrative team committed to a professional learning community that emphasizes anti-racism education as a pedagogy to achieve equity, diversity and social justice;
- the identification of mentor teachers to serve as role models for anti-racism educators;
- an organizational structure to accommodate a PD day and bi-weekly seminars about anti-racism education; and
- a structure and protocol whereby teacher candidates could learn about the community served by Maple Leaf School.

Four of the five teacher candidates in this project "described themselves as coming from homogeneous white communities. Although three of these four had non-Anglo European heritage, they all understood themselves to be part of the dominant culture. The other student described herself as being in one of the few black families in a homogeneous white community" (Norquay 1996, 6). Further demographic profiling revealed these teacher candidates to be from middle class, English-speaking families.

Norquay's study indicates that Maple Leaf School was the candidates' first encounter with student diversity and a school environment and curriculum that reflected this diversity. The following interview excerpts indicate the TCs' initial responses to an anti-racism school environment:

Well, it was culture shock... . I come from a very suburban area... . It was mostly Italian Canadian kids [living there]. (Norquay, 6)

I already had some idea of what to expect because [our Adjunct Professor] had talked to us about anti-bias [curriculum] prior to our [first] meeting at the school... . So I was thinking 'anti-bias', like, all over the place; on the walls, really overblown... . But it was more what was done; ... more action instead of just what you [might] see in a school. (Norquay, 6)

On Becoming Anti-Racism Educators

To provide teacher candidates with role models, the school administrators identified three teachers who could articulate as well as practice good anti-racism teaching. These practitioners became key personnel in building a partnership with teacher educators in facilitating an equity-based practicum environment. They articulated the following key factors generally associated with anti-racism teaching practice:

- developing and nurturing the self-esteem of students;
- the inclusion of representations of the genders and races of students in the curriculum;
- the inclusion of students' cultures and religions in the curriculum;
- setting high academic expectations for students; and
- helping students deal with conflict. (Norquay, 4)

To achieve the aims shown above, these anti-racism educators had to reveal their own professional development journeys: attend anti-racism workshops offered by the school district and school; learn how to critically evaluate for bias learning materials in the school library; purchase appropriate "multicultural" books; and visit public libraries in the community in search of additional resources. Most important for these anti-racism educators was self-interrogation for their own biases, prejudices and assumptions. Norquay reported a teacher as saying, "We have to bring [our] biases to the fore and be able to stand up and be counted" (5). This was believed to be "a fundamental underpinning of successful antiracism teaching" (5).

Community Explorations for TCs

An important dimension of the Maple Leaf professional learning model is familiarity with and knowledge of the community served by the school. Educators have emphasized this knowledge as key to providing "culturally relevant pedagogy" (Ladson-Billings 1995). More and more, progressive teacher educators in partnership with their practicum schools are developing creative involvement of teacher candidates (as well as veteran teachers) in the life of their students' communities (See Chapter 7 for the theory and practise of community involvement).

To facilitate this community exploration process, the Maple Leaf School administration arranged a walking tour for TCs of the community in which the school is located. The following is a checklist of activities summarized from McKeown's Maple Leaf Community Profile:

- survey where students live and record the streets and areas in which they live ;
- visit shopping areas and speak with proprietors about the demographics of their clients/customers;
- survey the faith and religious institutions in the community and investigate who their congregation might be; and
- visit community centre or park and recreation services to ascertain what resources, services, or programs are available to residents.

Norquay's study (11) captures some of the TCs' insights from these explorations, as evidenced in the following:

> It's terrible to say, but I've never really thought of the community. Of course, it's a part of the school, but never to the extent that Maple Leaf [makes it]. The community's everything. The school boundaries don't end.

Bi-Weekly Seminars

The goal of these seminars was to increase informed dialogue among the "community of learners": teacher candidates, veteran teachers and teacher educators. Cochran-Smith and Lytle (1993) have documented this approach to collaborative PD.

The seminar discussions were generated from the research literature on social justice, equity and diversity education and aspects of teaching and learning, and facilitated by the school's Vice Principal, who was also the Adjunct

Professor.[4] Initially, the PD plan was for TCs and mentor teachers to read and discuss the assigned articles in preparation for seminars that took place during class time.

Although these sessions provided the opportunity for TCs to connect with each other, reflect upon the readings and broaden their knowledge base, unfortunately the mentor teachers were not released from their classroom duties to participate in them.

Despite this missing dimension to the seminar discussions, TCs gained useful awareness and knowledge as is reported here:

> I wasn't really aware of multiculturalism and anti-bias curriculum and how important it is... I've been told so much about it but I've never really seen it written down or used in an example... . I thought it was good to start with the articles rather than just jumping into the classroom and not knowing if I should be doing this or that. (Norquay, 12).

To conclude, the Maple Leaf model for building a professional learning community revealed some critical dimensions: strong, involved leadership, key exemplars of equity education, community exploration by TCs to ensure culturally-relevant pedagogy, and a schedule of regular seminars. The challenge that presented itself for this model was providing the logistical arrangements and resources required to include mentor teachers in the seminars.

THE PEEL-UNIVERSITY PARTNERSHIP MODEL[5]

The Nahani Way Public School project grew out of a larger Peel School District-University partnership that brought together teacher practitioners, teacher candidates, school district professional development personnel and teacher educators from the university. The goal of the project was to create a culture of learners that generated professional growth of teachers. Such growth, in turn, led to improved classroom pedagogy and teaching to students of an equitable and diverse nature.

Key features of this initiative were:

- the provision of professional development time within the teaching day;
- collaborative action research and classroom inquiry;
- sharing and dissemination of professional learning; and
- professional growth plans and portfolio documentation.

PD During Teaching Day

Through a high level of teacher commitment and collaboration, creative timetabling, and administrative leadership and support, teams of teachers at the Nahani Way school were able to spend time out of their classrooms engaged in activities designed to improve their practice. Logistical arrangements made it possible for teams numbering from 4 to 6 teachers to be scheduled for PD projects in 80-minute blocks once per month from October to May 1997–98. This arrangement utilized such professional support staff as librarians and the administrative team, and provided the opportunity for all classroom teachers to participate in this PD initiative without the loss of lunch periods, after-school preparation time, or extra-curricular activities time.

Collaborative Action Research Classroom Inquiry

Teams of teachers developed their own action research projects based on classroom needs. The following are areas of inquiry that emerged:

- Student talk and teacher talk: questioning
- Assessment
- Emergent and early literacy
- Developmentally appropriate practice
- Math, Science and Technology
- Program diversification to ensure student success
- Integrating computers into meaningful classroom practice

The action research process utilized in exploring these job-embedded areas is well documented in many field-based research guides (e.g., *Field-based research: A working guide*, British Columbia Ministry of Education & Multiculturalism and Human Rights 1992). Generally, the action research process included:

- identifying issues, problems or questions to be explored;
- developing a research plan to collect the data;
- implementing the plan of action;
- collecting data generated by the plan of action;
- analyzing, reflecting, theorizing about the findings; and
- modifying and redefining the question or concern and continuing the next round of action research or classroom inquiry.

Methods of collecting data for this professional dialogue included:

- notes from classroom participant and non-participant observation;
- audio and video recordings;
- student work samples, e.g., writing, art, maintaining a journal or log; and
- articles or materials read and collected from professional journals.

An essential dimension of this collaborative action research process was the sharing, reflection and professional learning that took place in the course of teachers and facilitators meeting regularly to discuss their classroom inquiry. In monthly meetings each research team provided a progress report on a project. Collected data included samples of student work that were relevant to their study, e.g. language, art, math, science; audio or video recordings of classroom or field trip interaction; samples from a field trip, etc. Other teams that were further along the path of inquiry engaged each other and the facilitators in an analysis and interpretation of data in an effort to interpret the meaning of their work. At the level of theory, yet other groups brought in readings that were relevant to their project, culled from the research literature.

The end product of this inquiry was the improvement of classroom pedagogy, but the process was highly collaborative. The essence of such collaboration and sharing is captured in this teacher participant's reflection:

Job embedded, school-based professional development provides both framework and a discipline for my learning. It is more formal and more focused. Discussions and reflections make visible and raise my awareness of the complexity of children's learning. I get so involved in the day-to-day running of the classroom, at times "I can't see the forest for the trees." There is no chance to reflect. One becomes reactive instead of proactive. When I have an audience, I have a reason for my research. My colleagues become my sounding boards and my research goes beyond myself. I have a reason for writing. Talking with one another allows for different perspectives and different interpretations of information. As a group we go beyond anything an individual could do on her own. We are examining our practice in light of our theories of education. By doing this our practice changes our theories and our theories change our practice. (Barbara, *Action Research Team: Developmentally Appropriate Practice*)

Some Positive Outcomes

The Nahani Way professional learning community provided the opportunities for teachers to methodically investigate their classroom teaching and learning. This, indeed, led to improved pedagogical practices. Also, the collaborative approach to classroom inquiry built connections with colleagues within the school and with other professionals in partner institutions. Finally, teachers developed professional growth plans and documented their growth experiences in their professional portfolios. This is significant in their quest as "life-long learners."

Sharing of PD Initiatives

The following are specific sharing activities in which Nahani Way [school] teachers engaged during the life of the project.

Celebration of Professional Growth: Sharing Your Learning
A special staff meeting close to the end of the school year was set aside for the action research teams to display and share their projects with other members of the school community. Guiding this sharing session were the following questions:

- What is your research question, focus, or issue?
- What did you do? Describe the process, the method of collecting data.
- What did you find out?
- How did this improve or change your practice?

This session was documented on videotape for the future use of teachers or PD Planners.

Professional growth through connections
Let's talk literacy: Sharing stories from our classroom. This was a workshop series hosted by Nahani Way for classroom teachers to share and reflect upon such literacy issues as journals and early writing, portfolios, developing a novel program, computers and writing, literature circles, writing and students with learning disabilities, developmentally-appropriate practice in early childhood, action research about literacy, and homework. Participating teachers were from Nahani Way and the Lyndwood family of schools.

Sharing with School Board-University Partners

Representatives of action research teams had the opportunity to present their projects to the school district administrative team (including the Director and Associate Director), and to administrative teams of partner universities— York University and the Ontario Institute for the Study of Education-University of Toronto. These administrators gained valuable insights into ways in which learning communities can be creatively structured to facilitate teachers' PD and student learning, and shared these insights with their constituencies.

The Video Journal of Education

This is a series of staff development videotapes that highlight current research and innovative classroom practices for school reform and improvement. Nahani Way teachers were identified as highly successful in their PD model and were featured in Michael Fullan's and Andy Hargreaves' video program based on the *What's Worth Fighting For* trilogy. The Video Journal of Education has a wide circulation and is used by school districts and teacher educators throughout the United States, Canada and other parts of the world.

The following reflection captures the PD coordinator's enthusiasm for the school's recognition:

> The Video Journal of Education came to Nahani Way to videotape several teacher along with their students, in their classrooms where innovative and successful practices were being used... . One of our action research groups demonstrated the collaborative process that took place during our professional growth discussions. I felt that this was a unique area of strength in our school that would be helpful to other educators as we all move forward in school improvement and reform... . [This is] an exciting opportunity to celebrate our successes with a very broad audience!
>
> (Linda Richardson, PD coordinator)

Some Challenges

The most unique feature of the Nahani Way professional learning community, that is, releasing teachers from their classroom responsibilities to engage in action research, was also its biggest challenge. Although the school's administrative team did extensive planning and preparation to ensure adequate class coverage, unforeseen circumstances (e.g., teacher absence, urgent one-on-one attention to students experiencing problems, teacher re-assignment to other urgent school matters, unplanned meetings with parents, field trip coverage, etc.) would occasionally interrupt PD plans. Such eventualities and other calls of duty were also obstacles to action research progress.

This, therefore, is the dimension of the PD model that school districts and their school administrative teams must consider for additional resources.

AN EMERGENT "COMMUNITY OF LEARNERS" MODEL

From our analysis of the three variations of the "community of learners" model , some key factors have emerged that are essential in the productive functioning of a community— one where teacher candidates, mentor teachers and teacher educators engage in critical pedagogical work for the improvement of practice. These key factors are: progressive administrative leadership, the relaxation of school-university boundaries for stronger cross-institutional relationships, and the development of PDSs as sites of inquiry.

Progressive Administrative Leadership

Such communities require leaders that are resourceful, creative, dynamic, risk-taking, moral and visionary. The administrators in these models creatively reconceptualize professional learning as an activity unrestricted by one-day, one-shot PD days, lunchtimes and after school periods. As more demands are placed on teachers' classroom and non-teaching time, and policy makers reduce professional activity days, school leaders must demonstrate their resourcefulness by creating space for teacher development during the workday. These are leaders who are not preoccupied with bureaucratic plant management and maintenance. Instead, they tolerate instability, a breach of harmony, and some level of ambiguity, as the community reorganizes itself to maximize learning. McLaren and Dantley (1990, 40) urge us to generate the power to "move educational leadership from the sterile, passionless practice of antiseptic administration to a vigorous and impassioned mobilization for greater democracy, equality, and community."

Beyond providing the logistical arrangements for professional learning, such progressive school leaders have also taken strong, unwavering positions on school transformation. Solomon (2002, 194) argues:

Administrative neutrality may be the path of least resistance when working with divergent ideas, philosophies, and pedagogies within a school community. But taking a centrist position and implementing "soft" programs that do not interrogate deep-seated... ideologies that are imbedded in the cultural, social and economic structures of society will not be transformative.

PDS leaders must therefore be interventionists, taking risks and moving from a position of neutrality to critique structures that maintain inequities in society. They must use the power invested in their administrative leadership to effect institutional change.

Indeed, guiding a community of learners from the way things are to the way they ought to be requires vision. Here Foster (1989, 54) relates the challenges:

> This is perhaps the most crucial and critical role of leadership: to show new social arrangements, while still demonstrating a continuity with the past: to show how new social structures continue, in a sense, the basic mission, goals and objectives of traditional human intercourse, while still maintaining a vision of the future and what it offers.

PRODUCTIVE INSTITUTIONAL BORDER-CROSSING

Another essential dimension of an emergent community of learners model is creating a professional learning environment that provides easy access to the institutions in the partnership. Here the organizational arrangements between the university and practicum schools provide the conditions for participants to build fluid relationships with each other and engage meaningfully in each other's work setting.[6] Indeed, it is well documented in the research literature that university-school partnerships are fraught with challenges (Dagenais and Wideen 1999; Rolheiser 1999; Wideen and Lemma 1999). Conflicts and tensions are generated over issues of power, ownerships, territory, the nature of knowledge about teaching (Dagenais and Wideen); tensions occur around status and influence of participants; differential perspectives on change; and insider-outsider relationships (Rolheiser 1999). Alexander, Gerofsky and Wideen (1999, 229) alert us to the tendency of teacher candidates to be marginalized in teacher education reforms:

> The professional, academic and administrative discourses in teacher education can sometimes unintentionally overshadow the voices and experiences of the teacher candidates, particularly when administration and school partnerships occupy the stage in a more compelling manner.

In this emergent "community of learners" model, candidates are central, and are the vital link between the university and the school, the university lecture room and practicum classroom, the school and the community that it serves, and the university and the community it serves. Working effectively across these borders requires transforming the social relations and contesting the hierarchies that traditionally exist among these institutions and their agents. For the teacher candidate the most rigid border to negotiate may well be school cultures and the prescribed roles and relationships assigned to each member of the community (Menter 1989).

This chapter proposes a model that transcends "stasis" by creating an alternative learning environment where all partners in the practicum enterprise (TCs, mentor teachers and teacher educator) participate in structured, interactive experiences of collaborative resonance—a critical theory-based professional development approach that strives for educational equity and diversity in the PDS (see Figure 8.3).

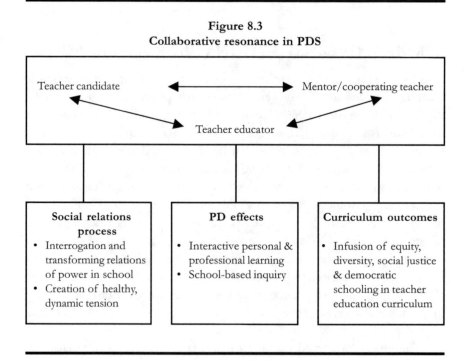

Figure 8.3
Collaborative resonance in PDS

PDSs as Sites of Inquiry

Emerging from the PDS models presented in this chapter is the theory and practice of school-based inquiry. Such an activity is variously labelled as "practitioner research," "action research," "school-based inquiry," "site-based research," "participatory research," and "teacher as researcher" approach. The Holmes Group (1990) calls the PDS "school as centres of inquiry."

This dimension of the emergent model emphasizes the power of moving beyond the uncritical acceptance of the status quo, the taken-for-granted assumptions about knowledge and its epistemology. PDS provides the environment for stakeholders in the schooling process to engage collaboratively in exploring schools and the communities they serve.

In the three cases presented here, we see teachers engaged in job-embedded inquiry designed to explore problematic realities of classrooms and schools, and to improve their pedagogy and their professional competence. We see teacher candidates engaged in community studies to ascertain the locality's needs and resources. The expectation is that the acquisition of such knowledge will help them engage in culturally-relevant pedagogy. Indeed, the beneficiaries of such inquiry are the students that come from these communities.

In their book: *Studying your own school: An educator's guide to qualitative practitioner research*, Anderson, Kerr and Nihlen (1994) provide some assumptions about practitioner research that reinforce the "community of learners" approach highlighted in this chapter. They perceive collaboration, empowerment and politics as key dimensions of school-based inquiry. Although they draw lines of demarcation between practitioner and academic research, they highlight the need for the dispassionate "outsider" to bring a more objective and critical perspective to the inquiry. The collaboration advocated in this chapter is one where teacher candidates and teacher educators, each bringing unique perspectives, experiences and skills to the research process, support teachers as insiders, and is one for whom the involvement achieves personal and professional objectives. Anderson et al. perceive this as "building collegiality and a common community of learning among practitioners, which in turn provides a model of inquiry for students" (7).

The issue of empowerment is key to research at the PDS level. This shift of the research process away from its traditional location in universities to the school setting empowers practitioners as creators of their own research knowledge. It demystifies the research process and makes it accessible to all collaborators.

Finally, research that critically examines issues of equity, diversity, social justice and democratic education is politically potent. Moving from institutional "stasis" to research synergy threatens those with a vested interest and ideological commitment to the way things are. With the advent of new ways of knowing, and the progressive pedagogies that support them (e.g., feminist and anti-racism pedagogies), subjugated knowledge, although resisted in conservative school cultures, is gaining legitimacy in emerging heterogeneous institutional settings. This makes the PDS and its learning community a rich terrain where traditional knowledge is contested and new research knowledge generated.

ENDNOTES

1. The representative for the Etobicoke Board of Education (now a part of the Toronto District School Board) in this partnership project was Goli Razai-Rashti. She was responsible for making the logistical arrangement for the seminars and providing the reading materials for the teacher participants in the project.
2. A research-teaching development grant from the [Ontario] provincial government (1994-1996) funded replacement (supply) teachers who released mentor teachers from their classes, in order to participate in these half-day workshops.
3. Information about this model was summarized from Naomi Norquay's (1996) study: *Teaching social equity in pre-service education through partnerships with schools; A report on the placement of Education I students at Maple Leaf Public School*. Unpublished Report, Faculty of Education, York University. Norquay was the teacher educator and practicum co-ordinator responsible for initiating, documenting and evaluating the project.
4. An Adjunct Professor (AP) in the practicum setting is an experienced teacher-practitioner who coordinates the in-school practicum and assists the practicum supervisor (the teacher educator from the University) in the supervision, mentoring and evaluation of teacher candidates.
5. Information for this section was gleaned from an extensive log of the Nahani Way Public School project: *Professional Growth of teachers: Creating a Culture of learners for school improvement (1998)*. Linda Richardson, Site Coordinator of the Peel-University Partnership, developed the log. She was the initiator and coordinator of the school's professional learning activities and also co-facilitated teacher research projects with Patrick Solomon (York University), and Paul Shaw (Peel District School Board).
6. In the York teacher education model, practicum school personnel such as the adjunct professor (AP) participate with the practicum supervisors in conducting seminars and performing other teaching functions for TCs in the university setting.

Impact of Teacher Identity on Perspectives and Practices

In this study, factors such as the school panel in which teachers work, their gender, their length of teaching experience and their heritage or ethnicity exert significant influence on their attitudes, beliefs, perspectives and practices of multicultural and anti-racist education. Teacher subgroups emerging from these biographical factors were matched with their perspectives on the following themes embedded in the 55-statement survey.

Participants responded concerning the goals and principles of multicultural and anti-racist education, and their level of acceptance:

- Policy implementation: the extent of implementation and the level of support for MCE and ARE policy within schools;
- The extent of integration of MCE and ARE into classroom teaching and other school practices;
- Beliefs (personal, pedagogical and political) and their compatibility with the goals of MCE and ARE; and
- The value and effectiveness of teacher education and professional development on MCE and ARE policy practice.

Statistically significant differences were found among survey respondents' subgroups and their perspectives on the above themes. The following are some of these differences.

SCHOOL PANEL

Elementary teachers (49.7% of respondents) were more positively disposed than their secondary counterparts to MCE and ARE (See Table A.1). Regarding school policy, elementary teachers were more critical of their schools for providing insufficient MCE and ARE resources and for incomplete implementation of policy. In teaching approaches and classrooms practices, elementary teachers were more likely to make connection between their students' lived experiences and the curriculum, and to integrate MCE and ARE resources into the mainstream curriculum. In their personal beliefs about pedagogy, elementary teachers were less inclined to believe that MCE and ARE lowered the quality of education. On the other hand, secondary school teachers were more in agreement than their elementary colleagues that "the school system functions successfully as it is; there is no need for MCE and ARE." Finally, regarding teacher education and professional development, elementary school teachers survey responses were more supportive of pre-and in-service programmes, taking more responsibility for changing teacher attitudes, behaviours, and institutional policies and practices which are discriminatory.

These findings reflect those of Echols and Fisher (1992) who found significant difference in elementary and secondary teachers' embrace of race-relations policy and its implementation. "Approximately twice as many elementary as secondary teachers report being involved in the development, revision or updating of the [action] plan" (67). As will be shown later, qualitative explorations into such dichotomous responses reveals that secondary school teachers' preoccupation with traditional pedagogic concerns and subject matter orthodoxy, reinforced by personal political stances on culture, race and the schooling process may have combined to marginalize MCE and ARE.

GENDER

Female respondents in the survey were more welcoming than their male counterparts to multicultural and anti-racist education (See Table A.2). Initially, both groups tended to agree that a goal of MCE is to encourage respect for a diversity of cultural traditions. However, when MCE objectives implied the integration of diverse norms, values and traditions into the mainstream curriculum, male teacher support fell. Female respondents were also more likely to integrate MCE and ARE into their classroom pedagogy and other school practices. Regarding other themes such as personal, pedagogical and political perspectives on MCE and ARE, and the value of teacher education and professional development on policy and its implementation, women's views were more positively-oriented than those of their male colleagues. There is a strong similarity of perspectives between females and elementary teachers. This similarity may be explained by the fact that elementary teachers in this study, and in the North American teaching profession at large, are predominantly female.

Table A.1
Teachers' Responses by School Panel

Survey Themes	School Panel	A. Mean	Std. Deviation	N
Policy implementation	Elementary	2.51	0.67	493
	Secondary	2.77	0.68	458
Supportive teaching practices	Elementary	2.01	0.50	497
	Secondary	2.26	2.26	463
Beliefs	Elementary	3.78	0.56	497
	Secondary	2.49	0.59	463
Value of teacher education and training	Elementary	2.34	0.54	497
	Secondary	2.49	0.59	463

Table A.2
Teachers' Responses by Gender

Survey Themes	B. Gender	Mean	Std. Deviation	N
Agreement with goals of MCE and ARE	Female	1.67	0.56	560
	Male	1.78	0.63	328
Supportive teaching practices	Female	2.01	0.67	463
	Male	2.30	0.50	497
Beliefs	Female	3.43	0.57	560
	Male	3.30	0.60	328
Value of teacher education and training	Female	2.32	0.52	560
	Male	2.54	0.59	328

LENGTH OF TEACHING EXPERIENCE

Respondents were fairly evenly distributed over six categories: 0 to 5 years, 6 to 10 years, 11 to 15 years, 16 to 20 years, 21 to 25 years, and 26 years and over. Of these categories, statistically significant differences were found most often between those with least (0 to 5 years) and the most (26 years and over) teaching experience, with the latter differentiating from other categories as well (See Table A.3).

Teachers with 26 years and more of teaching experience were less positive than their less experienced colleagues about the goals of MCE and ARE. They were also more likely to be satisfied with the level of policy implementation and the amount of resources allocated to MCE and ARE within their schools. The less experienced teachers, on the other hand, reported more often that they integrate MCE and ARE into all aspects of their classroom pedagogy and other school practices.

In ascertaining survey respondents' pedagogical and political beliefs, survey statements solicited whether MCE and ARE programs raised issues that were too sensitive for the classroom, overemphasized student differences at the expense of their similarities, alienated the dominant (white) groups in society, or were just another fashionable curriculum initiative. Again, those with more teaching experience, particularly 26 years and over, were more likely to agree with these negatively coded statements.

Finally, to the statement, "MCE and ARE school reforms are a threat to job security and seniority rights," veteran teachers concurred much more than their junior colleagues.

Table A.3
Teachers' Responses by Years of Teaching Experience

Survey Themes	Years of Teaching Experience	Mean	Std. Deviation	N
Satisfaction with policy implementation	0-5	2.76	0.67	185
	26+	2.48	0.58	178
Supportive teaching practices	0-5	2.16	0.67	187
	26+	3.22	0.59	179
Beliefs	0-5	3.52	0.54	187
	26+	3.22	0.59	179
Agreement with goals of MCE and ARE	21-25	1.61	0.56	168
	26+	1.88	0.68	178

HERITAGE AND ETHNICITY

Teachers' heritage and ethnicity significantly influenced their perspectives and practices of multicultural and anti-racist education (See Table A.4). The four major groups emerging were Canadian, British European, Continental European, and Racial Minority. Although the survey specifically requested respondents' heritage or ethnic affiliation (e.g. Asian-Canadian), the largest group (32.9%) resisted self-identity as hyphenated Canadians.[1]

A number of significant differences were found among the groups, but more specifically, between the Racial Minority and the Canadian groups. The cluster of survey statements that drew divergent responses were those that focused on teaching practices that explicitly favoured diversity in the classroom and integrated MCE and ARE into all subjects. These practices favoured the development of students as activists, working for social justice within their schools and communities. Racial minorities were much more supportive of these statements than the Continental European and the Canadian groups. The latter was also inclined to express the pedagogical and political beliefs that MCE and ARE lowered the quality of education, were less important than literacy and numeracy skills, and resulted in "reverse discrimination." The beliefs of the racial minority group were more compatible with the goals of MCE and ARE.

On the survey statements that probed the importance of pre-service and in-service teacher education for working in ethno-racially diverse classrooms, racial minorities and Continental Europeans attached more importance to such engagement than the Canadian group. The latter tended to favor classroom experience over education and training. Also, in response to the statement, "I believe some students are given limited educational opportunity because of their race/ethnicity," the British European group tended to agree more than the Canadian group.

These findings provide valuable insights into the polarized attitudes and perspectives of teachers differentiated by their heritage or ethnicity, and project serious implications for classroom practice. Similar research findings are emerging from the study of teaching in racialized societies such as the United States (Sleeter 1992a, 1993; King 1991), and Britain (Nehaul 1996; Troyna 1993; Figueroa 1991). In Canada, the Carr and Klassen (1997) study, for example, found that "white teachers are generally less supportive than their racial minority colleagues of antiracist education that attempts to shape the institutional culture of schools" (67). More specifically, these teacher groups differed in their perspectives on such issues as support for equity employment, racial minority teachers as role models (see also Solomon 1997, and Dei 1995), the role of the principal in supporting anti-racism, and the treatment of racial minority teachers (67).

Table A.4
Teachers' Responses by Heritage/Ethnicity

Survey Themes	Heritage/Ethnicity	Mean	Std. Deviation	N
Supportive teaching practices	Racial Minority	1.93	0.60	80
	Canadian	2.23	0.59	329
Beliefs	Racial Minority	3.85	0.54	81
	Canadian	3.54	0.63	329
Value of teacher education and training	Racial Minority	2.17	0.54	81
	Canadian	2.53	0.57	329

The findings of this study, supported in part by the research literature, have highlighted how teachers' locations within the hierarchical structure of schools (for example, in elementary and secondary teaching panels, and on the seniority continuum) and in the larger gender and ethnic-stratified society may influence their perspectives and practices of multicultural and anti-racist education. We concur with Sleeter (1992b) that race, gender and social class locations have far reaching consequences for the schooling process in diverse societies.

ENDNOTES

1. Teachers expressed their resistance to identification by heritage or ethnicity in many ways. The following are some of the responses written into the space provided for heritage/ethnicity information:
    - "Canadian-Canadian"
    - "Canadian by Nature."
    - "CANADIAN !!!!"
    - "Canadian first; no hyphen please."
    - "I disagree; should not use hyphenated descriptions."
    - "[Hyphenation] Not appropriate; I am a Canadian."
    - "This [heritage/ethnicity identity] should have no bearing at all; I refuse to answer."

appendix b

The Multiculturalism Policy of Canada

It is hereby declared to be the policy of the Government of Canada to:

(a) recognize and promote the understanding that multiculturalism reflects the cultural and racial diversity of Canadian society and acknowledges the freedom of all members of Canadian society to preserve, enhance and share their cultural heritage;

(b) recognize and promote the understanding that multiculturalism is a fundamental characteristic of the Canadian heritage and identity and that it provides an invaluable resource in the shaping of Canada's future;

(c) promote the full and equitable participation of individuals and communities of all origins in the continuing evolution and shaping of all aspects of Canadian society and assist them in the elimination of any barrier to such participation;

(d) recognize the existence of communities whose members share a common origin and their historic contribution to Canadian society, and enhance their development;

(e) ensure that all individuals receive equal treatment and equal protection under the law, while respecting and valuing their diversity;

(f) encourage and assist the social, cultural, economic and political institutions of Canada to be both respectful and inclusive of Canada's multicultural character;

(g) promote the understanding and creativity that arise from the interaction between individuals and communities of different origins;

(h) foster the recognition and appreciation of the diverse cultures of Canadian society and promote the reflection and the evolving expressions of those cultures;

(i) preserve and enhance the use of languages other than English and French, while strengthening the status and use of the official languages of Canada; and

(j) advance multiculturalism throughout Canada in harmony with the national commitment to the official languages of Canada.

Excerpts from the *Canadian Multiculturalism Act*, July 1988

Teaching for Equity and Diversity

appendix c

School Boards' Policies

	School Board 1	School Board 2	School Board 3	School Board 4	School Board 5
Introduction and Overview	Commitment to race relations, cross cultural Understanding and human rights	The Board develops and promotes racial harmony among students, staff and within the community.	Positive race and ethnic relations and communicate this commitment to everyone, and to take appropriate action when necessary.	Extensive look at the development of the policy and community involvement. Creation of a task force made up of trustees, administrators, educators and community members.	Policy of non-discrimination shall prevail in all board matters. Will uphold the Charter of Rights and Freedoms.
Harassment and Racial Issues	Opposes and will not tolerate any form of racial or ethnic harassment by its students, staff, board members or trustees	Condemns and refuses to tolerate expression of racial or ethnic bias in any form by students staff or trustees. (Provincial Human Rights Code; Canadian Bill of Rights and Statutory Powers Procedure Act.	Refusal to accept any form of racial or ethnic bias by staff students, trustees and visitors. Suggests expulsion or dismissal from position if such comments persist.	All human beings are born free and equal in dignity and rights. Discriminatory incidents involving students, parents and visitors, and staff, will be dealt with accordingly.	Will tolerate no discrimination on the basis of race, religion, colour, age, marital status, sex, ancestry, place of origin or political belief.

	School Board 1	School Board 2	School Board 3	School Board 4	School Board 5
Curriculum and Learning Resources	Materials - free from stereotypes based on race, culture, ethnicity, gender, religion, or disability. All learning resources provide students with the opportunities to develop positive racial and cultural, diversity, and promote the self-esteem of the individual.	Provide opportunity for children to develop positive attitude and absence of stereotyping based on race, colour, religion or ancestry. Student Programmes – to assist in developing a positive self-image and promote harmonious human relations.	Develop programmes and supply learning materials which promote self-esteem, pride in one's own culture, and positive attitudes towards people of all racial and ethnic backgrounds. Co-curricular activities and programmes that enhance personal development, social skills and harmonious race relations.	Extensive examination of the current resources and programmes, and implementation of inclusive and non-discriminatory curriculum that promotes the development of critical thinking skills.	Resources to support MCE and reflect cultural and ethnic diversity; must be designed to combat racism and prejudice.
Student Assessment and Placement	Ensures that all students have equal opportunity and be encouraged to fully participate in programmes.	Development of culturally appropriate testing instruments; increased efforts to inform parents about students' assessments.	Ensure that assessment and placement practices are sensitive to the racial, ethnic and educational backgrounds of its students. Will consider a 7-year adjustment period for newcomers.	Addressed in the Curriculum section. Evaluation based on whether current methods are free of bias.	

	School Board 1	School Board 2	School Board 3	School Board 4	School Board 5
Staff Development	On-going provisions of staff development	Implement in-service training for all staff in the school.	Equip employees with the awareness, knowledge and skills necessary for interacting with people of different racial and ethnic backgrounds.	Policy on career development, in-service and pre-service training as well as a section on Staff Development on its own.	Provide in-service training for MCE; principals encouraged to provide the same for groups specific to the school population.
Personnel Policies and Practices	All employees of the Board are aware of the policy and aims to achieve equity in employment.	Ensures that personnel will be aware of all relevant policies.	Ensures that personnel will be aware of all relevant policies.	Ensures that personnel will be aware of all relevant policies.	Denounces discrimination on behalf of all teachers in the board district.
School and Community Relations	Increased constructive and open dialogue with community (parents, other residence and businesses)	Encourage participation and greater cooperation of parents and community in the school	Promote Partnership between school and community. Attempt to decrease language barrier to do so effectively.	Addresses community involvement, role of parents in the educational process, communication with parents, and community agencies.	Commitment to the establishment of good relations and the removal of language barriers.

	School Board 1	School Board 2	School Board 3	School Board 4	School Board 5
	Treats all job applicants and employees without prejudice or discrimination on any grounds prohibited by the Human Rights Act.	Affirmative action policy leading to equal opportunities in employment and promotion in the Board.	Recruit, assign and promote on the basis of merit and in accordance with the Provincial Human Rights Code and Canadian Charter of Rights.	Includes a demand for staff and resources to manage the Employment Equity Programme and eliminate discriminatory barriers.	Discrimination prohibited. Give to all the opportunity for growth and advancement.
Equal Employment Opportunity	Priority Objectives and Strategies – implement programme that is learner-centred and structure that is accountable. • Also focus on needs of adult learner. • Guarantees implementation and evaluation of the policy		Implementation and Review - inform all staff of the intentions of the policy and provide appropriate resources. Review process includes the establishment of a committee to review briefs from employees, students, parents and community.	Built into all sections of the policy are the establishment of committees required to evaluate current policies and amend or create new ones	

School Board 1	School Board 2	School Board 3	School Board 4	School Board 5
School Visitors – principals refuse to admit person, group, or association whose intent it is to preach discrimination on the basis of colour, nationality, or place of origin.			Encourages the development of a policy for the selection of non-offensive school speakers and visitors – in the Curriculum section of the policy.	
			Race Relations Position – Coordinator selected to administer the implementation of the policy and seek to foster change. – Ongoing assessment and yearly reports.	

School Board 1	School Board 2	School Board 3	School Board 4	School Board 5
			Aboriginal Issues – Directly addresses the concerns of Aboriginal citizens with respect to staffing, consultative processes, writer in residence, ethno-demographic data, Aboriginal Literature, aboriginal issues: endorsement of existing programmes and Aboriginal languages.	
			School Prayers - in the curriculum section, eliminate formal school prayers and addresses the teaching of religion in general.	

School Board 1	School Board 2	School Board 3	School Board 4	School Board 5
			School Management - in the Curriculum section, directly addresses an examination of the Hidden Curriculum and its elimination.	
			Co-Curricular Activities section included in the Curriculum component of the policy.	Inter-cultural Education – promotion of cultural contact for students and student-directed inquiry into issues of multiculturalism and race relations.

Teaching for Equity and Diversity

References

Aboud, F. E. 1988. *Children and prejudice*. Oxford: Blackwell.

Aboud, F. and Doyle, A. 1996. Does talk of race foster prejudice or tolerance in children. *Canadian Journal of Behavioural Science*, 28: 161-170.

Acker, S. 1988. Teachers, gender and resistance. *British Journal of Sociology of Education*, 9: 307-322.

Adkins, A. and Hytten, K. 2000, April. Thinking through a pedagogy of whiteness: How studies of whiteness can enhance teacher preparation for culturally diverse classrooms. Paper presented at the annual meeting of the American Educational Research Association. New Orleans, LA.

Agocs, C., and Jain, H. 2001. *Systemic racism in employment in Canada: Diagnosing systemic racism in organizational culture*. Toronto: The Canadian Race Relations Foundation.

Ahlquist, R. 1992. Manifestation of inequality: Overcoming resistance in a multicultural foundations course. In *Researcher and multicultural education: From the marginal to the mainstream*, ed. Carl Grant, 89-105. London: Falmer.

Alba, Richard. 1999. Immigration and the American realities of assimilation and multiculturalism. *Sociological Forum*, 14(1): 3-25.

Alexander, K., Gerofsky, S. and Wideen, M. 1999. Towards an ecology of change. In *Ground level reform in teacher education: Changing schools of education*, ed. M. Wideen and P. Lemma, 215-231. Calgary: Detselig Enterprises.

Aljose, S.A. and Joyner, V.G. 1990. Cooperative learning: The rebirth of an effective teaching strategy. *Educational Horizons*, Summer: 197-202.

Alladin, M.I. 1996. *Racism in Canadian schools*. Toronto: Harcourt Brace & Co.

Allcott, T. 1992. Anti-racism in education: The search for policy-in-practice. In *Racism and education: Structures and strategies*, ed. D.Gill, B. Mayor, and M. Blair, 169-184. London: Sage Publications.

Allport, G.W. 1954. *The nature of prejudice*. Cambridge, MA: Addison Wesley.

Anderson, G.L., Kerr, K. and Nihlen, A. S. 1994. *Studying your own school: An educator's guide to qualitative practitioner research*. Thousand Oaks, Calif.: Corwin Press.

Bagley, C.A. 1992. In service provision and teacher resistance to whole-school change. In *Racism and education: Structures and strategies*, ed. D. Gill, B. Mayor, and M. Blair, 226-247. London: Sage Publications.

Banks, J.A. 2001. *Cultural diversity and education: Foundations, curriculum, and teaching*. 4th ed. Boston: Allyn and Bacon.

Beach, D. 1999. The problems of education change: working from the ruins of progressive education. *Scandinavian Journal of Educational Research*, 43(3): 231-247.

Beane, J.A. 1990. *Affect in the curriculum: Toward democracy, dignity, and diversity*. New York: Routledge.

Ben-Tovim, G., Gabriel, J., Law, I. and Stredder, K. 1991. A political analysis of local struggles for racial equality. In *Racism and antiracism: Inequalities, opportunities and policies*, ed. P. Braham, A. Rattansi, and R. Skellington, 201-217. London: Sage Publications.

Berlak, A. 1989. Teaching for outrage and empathy in the liberal arts. *Educational Foundations*, 3:69-93.

Beyer, L. 1987. What knowledge is of most worth in teacher education? In *Educating teachers: Changing the nature of pedagogical knowledge*, ed. J. Smyth, 19-34. London: Falmer Press.

Blauner, R. 1989. *Black lives, white lives: Three decades of race relations in America*. Berkeley: University of California Press.

———. 1972. *Racial oppression in America*. New York: Harper & Row.

Bolaria, B.S. and Li, P.S. 1988. *Racial oppression in Canada*. Toronto: Garamond Press.

Boothe, M., Furlong, J. and Wilkins, M. ed. 1990. *Partnerships in initial teacher training*. Cassell: London.

Boyle-Baise, M., and Efiom, P. 2000. The construction of meaning: Learning from service learning. In *Integrating service learning and multicultural education in colleges and universities*, ed. C. R. O'Grady, 209-226. Mahwah, New Jersey: Lawrence Erlbaum Associates.

British Columbia Ministry of Education & Multiculturalism and Human Rights 1992. *Field-based research: A working guide*.

Bullivant, M.B. 1989. Culture: It's nature and meaning for educators. In *Multicultural education: Issues and perspectives*, ed. J. Banks and C. Banks, 27-45. Boston: Allyn & Bacon.

Cabello, B. and Burstein, N.D. 1995. Examining teachers' beliefs about teaching in culturally diverse classrooms. *Journal of Teacher Education*, 46(4): 285-294.

Canada. Manpower and Immigration. 1975. *Green Paper on Immigration and Population.* Ottawa.

Carlson Learning Company. 1996. *Discovering Diversity Profile.* Minneapolis, MN.

Carr, P.R. and Klassen, T.R. 1997. Different perceptions of race in education: Racial minority white teachers. *Canadian Journal of Education*, 22(1): 67-81.

Carr, W. and Hartnett, A. 1996. *Education and the struggle for democracy: The politics of educational ideas.* Buckingham: Open University Press.

Chatter, N. 1996. *Re-viewing 'colour blindness': Implications for anti-racist educational praxis.* Unpublished paper, Department of Curriculum, Ontario Institute for Studies in Education/University of Toronto, Toronto.

Choney, S., Berryhill-Paapke, E. and Robbins, R.R. 1995. The acculturation of American Indians: Developing frameworks for research and practice. In *Handbook of multicultural counseling,* ed. J. G. Ponterotto, J. M. Casas, L. A. Suzuki, and C.M. Alexander, 73-92. Thousand Oaks, CA: Sage.

Clarke, R.W. 1999. *Effective professional development schools.* San Francisco: Jossey-Bass.

Cochran-Smith, M. 2000. Blind vision: Unlearning racism in teacher education. *Harvard Educational Review*, 70(2):157-190.

Cochran-Smith, M. 1995. Colourblindness and basket making are not the answers: Confronting the dilemmas of race, culture and language diversity in teacher education. *American Educational Research Journal*, 32(3): 493-522.

Cochran-Smith, M. and Lytle, S.L. ed. 1993. *Inside/outside: Teacher research and knowledge.* New York: Teachers College Press.

Connell, R.W. 1992 January. *Citizenship, social justice & curriculum.* Paper presented to the International Conference on Sociology of Education, Westhill, UK.

Connolly, P. 1992. *Press coverage of murder in the playground.* Unpublished master's thesis, University of Warwick, Coventry, UK.

Corbett, H.D., Firestone, W.A. and Rossman, G. 1987. Resistance to planned change and the sacred in school cultures. *Educational Administration Quarterly*, 23(4): 36-59.

Cross, W.E. 1971. The Negro-to-Black conversion experience: Toward a psychology of Black liberation. *Black World*, 20:13-27.

Crozier, G. and Menter, I. 1993. The Heart of the matter? Student teachers' experiences in school. In *Race, gender and the education of teachers,* ed. I. Siraj-Blatchford, 94-108. London: Open University Press.

Curtis, B., Livingstone, D.W., and Smaller, H. 1992. *Stacking the deck: The streaming of working-class kids in Ontario schools*. Toronto: Our School/Our Selves Education Foundation.

Dagenais, D. and Wideen, M. 1999. Teacher education at Simon Fraser University: Collaboration between professional cultures. In *Ground level reform in teacher education*, ed. M. Wideen and P. Lemma, 169-183. Calgary: Detselig Enterprises.

Dei, G.J.S. 1993. The challenges of antiracist education in Canada. *Canadian Ethnic Studies,* 25(2): 36-51.

_____. 1994. Black youth and fading out of school. In *Debating dropouts: New policy perspectives*, ed. J. Gaskell and D. Kelly, 173-189. New York: Teachers College Press.

_____. 1996a. *Antiracism education: Theory and practice.* Halifax: Fernwood.

_____. 1996b. Black/African-Canadian students' perspectives on school racism. In *Racism in Canadian schools*, ed. I. Alladin, 42-61. Toronto: Harcourt Brace.

Dei, G.J.S. and Calliste, A. ed. 2000. *Power, knowledge and anti-racism education*. Halifax: Fernwood.

Dei, G.J.S., and Karumanchery, L.L. 2001. School reforms in Ontario: The 'marketization of education' and the resulting silence on equity. In *The erosion of democracy in education*, ed. J. Portelli and R. P. Solomon, 189-215. Calgary: Detselig Enterprises.

Delpit, L.D. 1995. *Other people's children: Cultural conflict in the classroom*. New York: The New Press.

_____. 1988. The silenced dialogue: Power and pedagogy in educating other people's children. *Harvard Educational Review*, 58: 280-298.

Department of Education and Science. 1985. *Education for all*. Final Report of the Committee of Inquiry into the Education of Children from Ethnic Minority Groups, Cmd 8273. United Kingdom.

Derman-Sparks, L. and Phillips, C.B. 1997. *Teaching/Learning anti-racism: A developmental approach*. New York: Teachers College Press.

Dewey, J. 1900. *The school and society/The child and the curriculum*. Chicago: University of Chicago Press.

Donaldson, K.B.M. 2001. *Shattering the denial: Protocols for the classroom and beyond*. Westport, CT: Bergin & Garvey.

Echols, F.H. and Fisher, D. 1992. School action plans and implementation of a district race relations policy. *Canadian Ethnic Studies*, 24(1): 58-78.

Erickson, F. 1986. *Tasks in times: Objects of study in a natural history of teaching*. East Lansing: Institute for Research on Teaching, Michigan State University.

Feagin, J.R. and Vera, H. 1995. *White racism: The basics*. New York: Routledge.

Figueroa, P. 1991. *Education and the social construction of race*. London: Routledge.

_____. 1999. Multiculturalism and anti-racism in a new era: A critical review. *Race ethnicity and Education*, 2(2): 281-301.

Fine, M., Weis, L., Powell, L.C. and Wong, L.M. ed. 1997. *Off white: Readings on race, power, and society*. New York: Routledge.

Fine, M. 1991. *Framing dropouts: Notes on the politics of an urban public high school*. Albany, NY: SUNY Press.

Foster, P. 1990. *Policy and practice in multicultural and anti-racist education: A case study of a multi-ethnic comprehensive school*. London: Routledge.

Foster, W. 1989. Toward a critical practice of leadership. In *Critical perspectives on educational leadership*, ed. J. Smyth, 39-62. London: The Falmer Press.

Freire, P. 1973. *Pedagogy of the oppressed*. (Translated by M.B. Ramos.) New York: Seabury Press.

Gardner, H. 1983. *Frames of mind: The theory of multiple intelligences*. New York: Basic Books.

_____. 1999. *Intelligence reframed: Multiple intelligences for the 21st century*. New York: Basic Books.

Genovese, E. 1974. *Roll, Jordan,[R]oll: The world the slaves made*. New York: Pantheon Books.

Gillborn, D. 1995. *Racism and antiracism in real schools*. Buckingham: Open University Press.

Gilroy, P. 1987. *There ain't no black in the union jack*. Chicago: University of Chicago Press.

Ginsburg, M.B. 1988. *Contradictions in teacher education and society: A critical analysis*. London: Falmer Press.

Giroux, H. 1983. *Theory and resistance in education: A pedagogy for the opposition*. New York: Bergin & Garvey.

_____. 1988. *Schooling and the struggle for public life: Critical pedagogy in the modern age*. Minneapolis: University of Minnesota Press.

_____. 1992. *Border crossings: Cultural workers and the politics of education*. New York: Routledge.

Glaser, B.G. and Strauss, L.A. 1967. *The discovery of grounded theory: Strategies for qualitative research*. Chicago: Aldine Publishing.

Glatthorn, A.A. 1987. Cooperative professional development: Peer centred options for teacher growth. *Educational Leadership*, 45(3): 31-35.

Gollnick, D.M. 1992. Understanding the dynamics of race, class, and gender. In *Diversity in teacher education*, ed. M. E. Dilworth, 63-78. San Francisco: Jossey-Bass.

Gordon, B. 1985. Teaching teachers: 'A nation at risk' and the issue of knowledge in teacher education. *Urban Review,* 17: 33-46.

Grant, C. and Secada, W.G. 1990. Preparing teachers for diversity. In *Handbook of research on teacher education,* ed. W.R. Houston, 403-422. New York: MacMillan.

Green, M. 1996. In search of critical pedagogy. In *Breaking free: The transformative power of critical pedagogy.* ed. P. Leistyna, A.Woodrum, and S. Sherblom, 13-30. Cambridge, MA: Harvard University Press.

Greenman, N.P., Kimmel, E.B., Bannan, H.M. and Radford-Curry, B. 1992. Institutional inertia to achieving diversity: Transforming resistance into celebration. *Educational Foundations,* 60: 89-111.

Guadarrama, I. 2000. The empowering role of service learning in the preparation of teachers. In *Integrating service learning and multicultural education in colleges and universities,* ed. C. R. O'Grady, 227-243. Mahwah, New Jersey: Lawrence Erlbaum Associates.

Hall, S. 1981. Teaching race. In *The school in the multicultural society: A reader,* ed. A. James and R. Jeffcoate, 58-70. London: Open University Press.

Hallinan, M.T. and Teixeria, R.A. 1987, August. Students' interracial friendships: Individual characteristics, structural effects and racial differences. *American Journal of Education,* 95(4):563-583.

Hamilton, M.L. 1996. Tacit messages: Teachers' cultural models of the classrooms. In *Teacher thinking in cultural context,* ed. F.A. Rios, 185-209. Albany, N.Y.: State University of New York Press.

Hargreaves, A. 1991. Contrived Collegiality: The micropolitics of teacher collaboration. In *The Politics of life in schools: Power, conflict, and cooperation,* ed. J. Blase, 46-72. London: Sage Publications.

Hartnett, A. and Carr, W. 1995. Education, teacher development and the struggle for democracy. In *Critical discourses on teacher development,* ed J. Smyth, 39-53. Toronto: OISE Press.

Hawkey, K. 1994. Peer support in a school-based initial teacher education course. In *Teacher Education reforms: The research evidence,* ed. I. Reid and R. Griffiths, 137-143. London: Paul Chapman.

_____. 1995, May-June. Learning from peers: The experience of student teachers in school-based teacher-education. *Journal of Teacher Education,* 46(3): 175-183.

Helms, J.E. 1984. Toward a theoretical model of the effects of race on counseling: A Black and White model. *Counseling Psychologist,* 12:153-165.

_____. 1995. An update of Helms' white and people of colour racial identity models. In *Handbook of multicultural Counseling,* ed. J.G. Ponterotto, J. M.

Casas, L. A. Suzuki, and C. M. Alexander, 181-198. Thousand Oaks, CA: Sage.

Henry, F., Tator, C., Mattis, W. and Rees, T. 1995. *The colour of democracy: Racism in Canadian society*. Toronto: Harcourt Brace.

Herrnstein, R.J. and Murray, C. 1995. *The bell curve: Intelligence and class structure in American life*. New York: Free Press.

Hirschfeld, L.1996. *Race in the making: Cognition, culture and the child's construction of human kinds*. Cambridge, M.A.: MIT Press.

Holmes Group. 1995. *Tomorrow's colleges of education*. East Lansing, MI.

_____.1990. *Tomorrow's schools: Principles for the design of professional development schools*. East Lansing, MI.

Hones, D. 1997, March. *Preparing teachers for diversity: A service learning approach*. Paper presented at the annual meeting of the American Educational Research Association, Chicago, IL.

Honeyford, R. 1986. Anti-racist rhetoric. In *Anti-racism: An assault on education and value*, ed. F. Palmer, 43-56. London: Sherwood Press.

Howard, G.R. 1999. *We can't teach what we don't know: White teachers, multicultural schools*. New York: Teachers College Press.

Howard, J.P.F. 1998. Academic service learning: A counter normative pedagogy. In *Academic service learning: A pedagogy of action and reflection*, ed. R.A. Rhoads and J.P.F. Howard, 21-29. San Francisco: Jossey-Bass Publishers.

Howard, J.P.F., ed. 1993. Praxis 1: *A faculty casebook on community service learning*. Ann Arbor. MI: University of Michigan Office of Community Service Learning Press.

Howey, R. 1999. Professional development schools: Looking ahead. *Peabody Journal of Education*, 74(3,4): 332-334.

James, C.E. 1995a. *Seeing ourselves: Exploring race, ethnicity and culture*. Toronto: Thompson Educational Publishing.

_____. 1995b. "Reverse racism": Students' response to equity programs. *Journal of Professional Studies*, 3(1):48-54.

Jackson, L.C. 1999. Ethnocultural resistance to multicultural training: students and faculty. *Cultural Diversity and Ethnic Minority Psychology*, 5(1): 27-36.

Jeevanantham, L.S. 2001. In search of 'cultures' for multicultural education. *Pedagogy, Culture & Society*, 9 (1): 45-56.

Jeffcoate, R. 1984. *Ethnic minorities and education*. London: Harper and Row.

Johnston, M. 1999. New shoes for teacher education: Trying on collaboration and rethinking diversity in urban schools. In *Ground level reform in teacher education: Changing schools of education*, ed. M. Wideen and P. Lemma, 95-117. Calgary: Detselig Enterprises.

Kahne, J. and Westheimer, J. 1996, May. In the service of what? The politics of service learning. *Phi Delta Kappan*, 593-599.

Kailin, J. 1989. Preparing urban teachers for schools and communities: An anti-racist perspective. *High School Journal*, 82(12): 80-87.

_____. 2002. *Antiracist education: From theory to practice*. New York: Rowman & Littlefield.

Kalbach, M.A. and Kalbach, W.E. 1999. Persistence of ethnicity and inequality among Canadian immigrants. *Canadian Studies in Population*, 26(1): 83-105.

Kim, J. 1981. The process of Asian American identity development: A study of Japanese American women's perceptions of their struggle to achieve personal identities as Americans of Asian ancestry. *Dissertation Abstracts International*, 42: 1551A (University Microfilm No. 81-18080).

King, J.E. 1991. Dysconscious racism: Ideology, identity, and the miseducation of teachers. *Journal of Negro Education*, 60(2): 133-146.

Kingsley, C.W. and McPherson, K. ed. 1995. *Enriching the curriculum through service learning*. Alexandria, VA: Association for Supervision and Curriculum Development.

Kitano, H.L. 1982. Mental health in the Japanese American community. In *Minority mental health*, ed. E. E. Jones and S. J. Korchin, 149-164. New York: Praeger.

Kluth, P. 2000. Community-referenced learning and the inclusive classroom. *Remedial and Special Education*, 21(1): 19-26.

Koli, W. 2000. Teaching in the danger zone: Democracy and difference. In *Democratic social education: Social studies for social change*, ed. D. W. Hursch and E. W. Ross, 23-42. New York: Falmer Press.

Ladson-Billings, G. 1995. Toward a theory of culturally relevant pedagogy. *American Educational Research Journal*, 32: 465-491.

Lave, J. 1991. Situating learning in communities of practice. In *Perspectives on socially shared cognition*, ed. L.B. Resnick, J.M. Leveine and S.D. Teasley, 63-82. Washington, D.C: American Psychological Association.

Lawrence, S.M. and Tatum, B.D. 1997. Teachers in transition: The impact of antiracist professional development on classroom practice. *Teachers College Record*, 99(1): 162-178.

LeCompte, M.D. and Preissle, J. ed. 1993. *Ethnography and qualitative design in educational research* 2nd ed. San Diego: Academic Press.

Lee, E. 1986. Anti-racist education. Interview. *Orbit*, 17: 5-7.

Lee, F.Y. 1991. *The relationship of ethnic identity to social support, self-esteem, psychological distress, and help-seeking behaviour among Asian American college students.*

Unpublished doctoral dissertation, University of Illinois, Urbana-Champaign.

Levin, B. 2000. Democracy and schools: For citizenship. *Education Canada*, 40(3): 4-7.

Levine, M. and Churins, E.J. 1999. Designing standards that empower professional development schools. *Peabody Journal of Education*, 74(3,4): 178-208.

Levine-Rasky, C. 1998. Preservice teacher education and the negotiation of social difference. *British Journal of Sociology of Education*, 19(1): 89-112.

_____. 2000a. The practice of whiteness among teacher candidates. *International Studies in Sociology of Education*, 10(3): 263-284.

_____. 2000b. Framing whiteness: Working through the tensions in introducing whiteness to educators. *Race Ethnicity and Education*, 3(3): 271-292.

Levine-Rasky, C. ed. 2002. *Working through whiteness*. Albany: SUNY Press.

Li, P.S. 1988. *Ethnic inequality in a class society*. Toronto: Wall and Thompson.

Lieberman, A. and Miller, L. 1990. Teacher development in professional practice schools. *Teachers College Record*, 92(1): 105-122.

Lincoln, Y.S. and Guba, E.G. 1985. *Naturalistic inquiry*. Beverly Hills, CA: Sage Publications.

Liston, D. and Zeichner, K.M. 1991. *Teacher education and the social conditions of schooling*. New York: Routledge.

Lynch, J. 1987. *Prejudice reduction and the schools*. London: Nichols Publishing.

Mansfield, E. and Kehoe, J. 1994. A critical examination of anti-racist education. *Canadian Journal of Education*, 19(4): 418-430.

McCarthy, C. 1990. *Race and curriculum: Social inequality and the theories and politics of difference in contemporary research on schooling*. London: Falmer Press.

McCarthy, C. and Crichlow, W. ed. 1993. *Race, identity and representation in education*. New York: Routledge.

McDiarmid, G.W. 1990. Challenging prospective teachers' beliefs during early field experience: A quixotic undertaking? *Journal of Teacher Education*, 41(3): 12-20.

_____. 1990. The liberal arts: Will more result in better subject matter understanding? *Theory-into-Practice*, 29(1): 21-29.

_____. 1992. What to do about differences? A study of multicultural education for teacher trainees in the Los Angeles unified school district. *Journal of Teacher Education,* 3(2): 83-93.

McDonald, I., Bhavani, T., Khan, L. and John, G. 1989. *Murder in the playground: The Burnage report*. London: Longsight Press.

McFaul, S.A. and Cooper, J.M. 1984, April. Peer clinical supervision: Theory vs. Reality. *Educational Leadership*, 41: 4-9.

McIntosh, P. 1989. White privilege: Unpacking the invisible knapsack. *Independent School*, 49(2): 31-36.

_____. 1990. *Interactive phases of curricular and personal re-vision with regard to race*. Working Paper No. 219. Wellesley, MA: Wellesley College, Centre for Research on Women.

McIntyre, A. 1997. *Making meaning of whiteness: Exploring racial identity with white teachers*. Albany: State University of New York Press.

McLaren, P. and Dantley, M. 1990. Leadership and a critical pedagogy of race: Cornel West, Stuart Hall and the prophetic tradition. *Journal of Negro Education*, 59(1): 29-44.

McLaren, P. and Torres, R. 1999. Racism and multicultural education: Rethinking "race" and "whiteness" in late capitalism. In *Critical multiculturalism: Rethinking multicultural and antiracist education*, ed. S. May, 42-76. Philadelphia: Falmer Press.

Menter, I. 1989. Teaching practice stasis: Racism, sexism and school experience in initial teacher education. *British Journal of Sociology of Education*, 10(4: 459-473.

Miller, J.L. 1993. Solitary spaces: Women, teaching, and curriculum. In *The centre of the web: Women and solitude*, ed. D. Wear, 245-252. Albany: State University of New York Press.

Mock, K.R. and Masemann, V. L. 1990. *Implementing race and ethnocultural equity policy in Ontario school boards*. Toronto: Ontario Ministry of Education.

Morrison, T. 1992. *Playing in the dark: Whiteness and the literary imagination*. New York: Vintage.

Narode, R., Rennie-Hill, L. and Peterson, K.D. 1994. Urban community study by preservice teachers. *Urban Education*, 29(1): 5-21.

National Indian Brotherhood 1972. *Indian Control of Indian Education*. Ottawa:The National Indian Brotherhood.

Nevarez, A.A., Sanford, J.S. and Parker, L. 1997. Do the right thing. *Journal for a Just and Caring Education*, 3 (2): 160-179.

Nieto, S. 1995. From brown heroes and holidays to assimilationist agendas: Reconsidering the critiques of multicultural education. In *Multicultural Education, Critical Pedagogy, and the politics of difference*, ed. C. E. Sleeter and P. L. McLaren, 191-220. Albany, NY: SUNY Press.

Norquay, N. 1996. *Teaching social equity in pre-service education through partnerships with schools: A report on the placement of Education 1 students at Maple Leaf Public School*. Unpublished Report. York University, North York, Canada.

Oakes, J. 1985. *Keeping track*. New Haven, CT: Yale University Press.

O'Grady, C.R. 2000. Integrating service learning and multicultural education: An overview. In *Integrating service learning and multicultural education in colleges and universities*, ed. C R. O'Grady, 1-19. Mahwah, New Jersey: Lawrence Erlbaum Associates.

Omi, M. and Winant, H. 1994. *Racial formation in the United States: From the 1960s to the 1990s*. 2nd ed. London: Routledge.

Ornstein, A.C. and Levine, D.U. 1989. *Foundations of education*. 4th ed. Boston: Houghton Mifflin.

Ouseley, H. 1992. Resisting institutional change. In *Racism and Education: Structures and Strategies*. ed. D. Gill, B. Mayor, and M. Blair, 119-133. London: Sage Publications.

Palmer, F. 1986. *Antiracism: An assault on education and value*. London: Sherwood Press.

Pendakur, K. and Pendakur, R. 1996. *Earnings differentials among ethnic groups in Canada*. Ottawa: Strategic Research and Analysis, Department of Canadian Heritage.

Portelli, J.P. 1996. Democracy in education: Beyond the conservative or progressive stances. *Inquiry: Critical Thinking Across the Disciplines*, 16(1): 9-21.

Portelli, J.P., and Solomon, R.P., ed. 2001. *Erosion of democracy in education: From critique to possibilites*. Calgary: Detselig Enterprises.

Quinn, L.F. and McKay, J.W. 1998. *Professional development outcomes of multiple student teacher placements within a university/school partnership*. Draft presented at the annual meeting of the American Educational Research Association [AERA], San Diego.

Radest, H. 1993. *Community service: Encounter with strangers*. Westport, CT: Praeger.

Rezai-Rashti, G. 1995. Multicultural education, anti-racist education, and critical pedagogy: Reflections on everyday practice. In *Anti-Racism, Feminism, and Critical Approaches to Education*, ed. R. Ng, P. Staton, and J. Scane, 3-19. Westport, CN: Bergin & Garvey.

Rhoads, R.A. and Howard, J. ed. 1998. *Academic service learning: A pedagogy of action and reflection*. San Francisco: Jossey-Bass Publishers.

Richardson, L. 1998. *Professional growth of teachers: Creating a culture of learners for school improvement, the Peel-University partnership*. Unpublished portfolio. Peel District School Board, Mississauga, Ontario.

Rios, F.A. ed. 1996. *Teacher thinking in cultural contexts*. Albany: SUNY Press.

Rizvi, F. 1993. Children and the grammar of popular racism. In *Race, identity and representation in education*, ed. C. McCarthy and W. Crichlow, 126-139. New York: Routledge.

Robertson-Baghel, M. 1998. *The social construction of racial identity of white student teachers and its impact on their learning to teach.* Unpublished Master's thesis. York University, North York, Canada.

Rolheiser, C.1999. Redesigning teacher education: The delicate, demanding dance of "Ready, Fire, Aim." In *Ground level reform in teacher education*, ed. M. Wideen and P. Lemma, 119-148. Calgary: Detselig Enterprises.

Roman, L. 1993. White is a colour! White defensiveness, postmodernism, and anti-racist pedagogy. In *Race, identity and representation in education*, ed. C. McCarthy and W. Crichlow, 71-88. New York: Routledge.

Ross, D. and Smith, W. 1992. Understanding preservice teachers' perspectives on diversity. *Journal of Teacher Education*, 43(2): 94-103.

Ross, D., Brownell, M., Sindelar, P. and Vandiver, F. 1999. Research from professional development schools: Can we live up to the potential? *Peabody Journal of Education*, 74(3,4): 209-223.

Rothenberg, J.J. 1997, March. *Preparing white teachers for urban schools: A compendium of research.* Paper presented at the Annual Meeting of the American Education Research Association, Chicago, IL.

Royal Commission on Learning. 1994. Report of the Royal Commission on Learning: For the love of learning (5 Volumes). Toronto: Government of Ontario.

Ruiz, A.S. 1990. Ethnic identity: Crisis and resolution. *Journal of Multicultural Counseling and Development,* 18: 29-40.

Sarup, M. 1991. *Education and the ideologies of racism.* Stoke-on-Trent, UK: Trentham Books.

Schecter, S., Solomon, R.P. and Kittmer, L. 2003. Integrating teacher education in a community-situated school agenda. In *Multilingual education in practice: Using diversity as a resource*, ed. S. Schecter and J. Cummins, 81-96. Portsmouth, NH: Heinemann.

Schick, C. 2000, February. By Virtue of Being White: Resistance in antiracist pedagogy. R*ace, Ethnicity and Education,* 3: 83-102.

Schofield, J.W. 1997. Causes and consequences of the colourblind perspective. In *Multicultural education: Issues and perspectives.* 3rd ed., ed. J. Banks and C. Banks, 251-271. Boston: Allyn & Bacon.

Schon, D. 1983. *The reflective practitioner: How professionals think in action.* New York: Basic Books.

Schwartz, W. 2000. *The impact of professional development schools.* ERIC Clearinghouse on Urban Education, Institute for Urban and Minority Education. Teachers College, Columbia University, New York.

Sears, A. 1991. Cultural pairing: Widening the cultural horizons of prospective teachers. *Multiculturalism,* 13(3): 10-15.

Short, G. 1992. Responding to racism in prospective teachers. *Journal of Education and Teaching*, 18(2):173-183.

Short, G. and Carrington, B. 1996. Anti-racist Education, Multiculturalism and the New Racism. *Educational Review*, 48(1): 65-77.

Slavin, R.E. 1983. *Cooperative Learning*. New York: Longman.

Sleeter, C.E., 1992a. *Keepers of the American Dream: A Study of staff development and multicultural education*. London: Falmer.

_____. 1992b. Resisting racial awareness: How teachers understand the social order from their racial, gender, and social class locations. *Educational Foundations*, 6: 7-32.

_____. 1993. How white teachers construct race. In *Race, identity and representation in education*. ed. C. McCarthy and W. Crichlow, 157-171. Routledge.

Sleeter, C. and Grant, C. 1988. An analysis of multicultural education in the United States. *Harvard Educational Review*, 57: 421-444.

_____. 1988. *Making choices for multicultural education*. Columbus: Merrill Publ. Co.

Solomon, R.P. 1992. *Black resistance in high school: Forging a separatist culture*. Albany: State University of New York Press

_____. 1995a, Spring. Why to teach from a multicultural and anti-racist perspective in Canada. *Race, Gender and Class: An Interdisciplinary and Multicultural Journal*, 2 (3): 49-66.

_____. 1995b. Beyond prescriptive pedagogy: Teacher in-service education for cultural diversity. *Journal of Teacher Education*, 46(4): 1-8.

_____. 1997. Race, role-modelling and representation in teacher education and teaching. *Canadian Journal of Education*, 22 (4): 395-410.

_____. 2000. Exploring cross-race dyads in learning to teach. *Teachers College Record*, 102 (6): 953-979.

_____. 2002. School leaders and antiracism: Overcoming pedagogical and political obstacles. *Journal of School Leadership*, 12(1): 174-197.

Solomon, R.P. and Allen, A.M. 2001. The struggle for equity, diversity and social justice in teacher education. In *The erosion of democracy in education: From critique to possibilities*, ed. J. Portelli and R. P. Solomon, 217-244. Calgary: Detselig Enterprises.

Solomon, R.P. and Levine-Rasky, C. 1994. *Accommodation and resistance: Educators' response to multicultural and antiracist education*. A report to the Federal Department of Canadian Heritage. North York: York University.

_____. 1996a. When principle meets practice: Teachers' contradictory responses to antiracist education. *The Alberta Journal of Educational Research*, 42(1): 19-33.

_____. 1996b. Transforming teacher education for an antiracism pedagogy. *The Canadian Review of Sociology and Anthropology,* 33(3):337-359.

Solorzano, D.G. and Yosso, T.J. 2001. From Racial Stereotyping and Deficit Discourse toward a Critical Race Theory in Teacher Education. *Multicultural Education,* 9(1): 2-8.

Stake, R.E. 1995. *The art of case study research.* Thousand Oaks: Sage Publications.

Stanfield, J.H. 1991. Racism in America and in other race-centred nation-states: Synchronic considerations. *International Journal of Comparative Sociology,* 32(3,4): 243-260.

Statistics Canada, 2003. Canada's ethnocultural portrait: The changing mosaic. Census: analysis series. Catalogue No. 96F0030XIE1008. Ottawa: Ministry of Industry.

Stelcner, M. and Kyriazis, N. 1995. An empirical analysis of earnings among ethnic groups in Canada. *International Journal of Contemporary Sociology,* 32: 41-79.

Strauss, L.A. 1987. *Qualitative research for social scientists.* New York: Cambridge University Press.

Symons, T. 1975. *To Know Ourselves.* Ottawa: Association of Universities and Colleges of Canada.

Su, J.Z.X. 1990. The function of the peer group in teacher socialization. *PhiDelta Kappan,* May:723-727.

_____. 1992. Sources of influence in preservice teacher socialization. *Journal of Education for Teaching,* 18(3): 239-258.

Tatum, B.D. 1992. Talking about race, learning about racism: The application of racial identity development theory in the classroom. *Harvard Educational Review,* 62(1): 1-24.

_____. 1997. *Why are all the Black kids sitting together in the cafeteria? and other conversations about race.* New York: Basic Books.

Tellez, K., Hlebowitsh, P.S., Cohen, M., and Harwood, P. 1995. Social service field experiences and teacher education. In *Developing multicultural teacher education curricula,* ed. J.M. Larkin and C.E. Sleeter, 65-78. Albany: State University of New York Press.

Thayer-Bacon, B.J. 1998. *Philosophy applied to education: Nurturing a democratic community in the classroom.* Columbus, Ohio: Merrill.

Thomas, B. 1984. Principles of anti-racist education. *Currents: Readings in Race Relations,* 2 (3): 20-24.

Thompson, C.E. and Carter, R.T. ed. 1997. *Racial identity theory: Applications to individual, groups and organizational interventions.* Mahwah, New Jersey: Lawrence Erlbaum.

Tom, A. R. 1999. How professional development schools can destabilize the work of the university faculty. *Peabody Journal of Education*, 74(3,4): 277-284.

Toms, M. and Scarr, M. 1993, June. *Educating student teachers to take action on issues of equity and social justice*. Paper presented to the Canadian Society for the Study of Curriculum, Ottawa, Ontario.

Troyna, B. 1987. Beyond multiculturalism: Towards the enactment of Anti-racist education in policy, provision and pedagogy. *Oxford Review of Education*, 13(3): 307-320.

_____. 1993. *Racism and education: Research perspectives*. Buckingham: Open University Press.

_____. 1994. The 'everyday world' of teachers? Deracialised discourses in the sociology of teachers and the teaching profession. *British Journal of Sociology of Education*, 15(3): 325-339.

Troyna, B. and Hatcher, R. 1992. *Racism in children's lives: A study of mainly white primary schools*. London: Routledge.

Troyna, B. and Williams, J. 1986. *Race, education and the state: The racialization of education policy*. London: Croom Helm.

Van der Post, Laurens. 1986. A walk with a white bushman. In *Conversation with Jean-Marc Pottiez* [memoir]. London: Chatto & Windus.

Verma, G.K. ed. 1993. *Inequality and teacher education: An international perspective*. London: Falmer Press.

Walker, J. 1987. *Race and the historian: Some lessons from Canadian policy*. Unpublished Paper presented at the Canada 2000 Conference, Ottawa.

Warren, J.T. 1999. Whiteness and cultural theory: perspectives on research and education. *Urban Review*, 31(2): 185-203.

Watson, B. 1995, May-June. Relinquishing the lectern: Cooperative learning in teacher education. *Journal of Teacher Education*, 46(3): 209-215.

Watters, J.J. and Ginns, I.S. 1997. *Peer assisted learning: Impact on self-efficacy and achievement*. Paper presented at the annual meeting of the American Educational Research Association, Chicago, Illinois.

Welch, S. 1990. *A feminist ethic of risk*. Minneapolis: Fortress Press.

Wellman, D.T. 1993. *Portraits of white racism*. 2nd ed. Cambridge, U.K.: Cambridge University Press.

Wideen, M. and Lemma, P. ed. 1999. *Ground level reform in teacher education: Changing schools of education*. Calgary: Detselig Enterprises.

Willis, P. 1977. *Learning to labour: How working class kids get working class jobs*. New York: Columbia University Press.

Winks, R. W. 1971. *The Blacks in Canada: A history*. New Haven: Yale University Press.

Winant, H. 1997. Behind blue eyes: Whiteness and contemporary U.S. racial politics. *New Left Review*, 225: 73-89.

Wood, P. 1985. Schooling in a democracy: Transformation or reproduction. In *Multiculturalism as an educational policy*, ed. F. Rizvi. Geelong, Victoria: Deakin University.

Yon, D.A. 2000. *Elusive culture: Schooling, race, and identity in global times*. Albany: State University of New York Press.

Zeichner, K. 1996. Educating teachers for cultural diversity. In *Currents of reform in preservice teacher education*, ed. K Zeichner, S. Melnick, and M. L. Gomez, 133-175. New York: Teachers College Press.

Zeichner, K. and Melnick, S. 1996. The role of community field experiences in preparing teachers for cultural diversity. In *Currents of reforms in preservice teacher education*, ed. K. Zeichner, S. Melnick, and M.L.Gomez, 176-196. New York: Teachers College Press.

Index

Teaching for Equity and Diversity

responses to professional
development, 64–70, 75
see also Teacher candidates
Tellez, Kip , 133
Thayer-Bacon, B.J., 110
Thomas, Barb., 6
Thompson, C.E., 91
Toms, M., 82
Troyna, Barry, 6, 22, 125

Urban Diversity Teacher Education
Program (York University) 12–13,
87–88, 160
and cross-race dyad partnerships,
109–127
and growth plans, 99–100
and participants' growth, 100
and post-program evaluations, 97
and pre-program baselining, 96–97
and Racial Identity Development
study 95–100
and the Etobicoke-University
Partnership model, 159–161
participants, 94–95
program design and implementation,
94–100
reflections on, 136–145
see also Cross-race dyad partnerships

Watson, B., 111
Welch, Sharon, 84
Wellman, David T., 125
White
and "Canadian" identity, 108n, 114
defensiveness, 26, 108
immigrants, 23
people, 39, 84, 90, 126
privilege, 89, 102
racial identity, 90–94, 101–102
racialization, 84
role-reversal, 38
teacher candidates, 101–102, 118,
119, 120, 124, 127ns
teachers, 22, 25, 125

Whiteness, 99, 100, 101
Willis, Paul, 8, 14n
Wood, Peter, 80

Yon, Dan, 117

Zeichner, Kenneth, 133, 134

AGMV Marquis

MEMBER OF SCABRINI MEDIA

Quebec, Canada
2003